Theory and Methodology of Tactical Asset Allocation

Wai Lee

Published by Frank J. Fabozzi Associates

To my mother,
my wife, Kar-Lai,
and my daughter, Vera,
with gratitude and love

© 2000 By Frank J. Fabozzi Associates
New Hope, Pennsylvania

ISBN: 1-883249-72-4

Table of Contents

Preface

This book is based on a series of research papers I wrote on tactical asset allocation. The seed for the book was planted in 1995 while I was working with Professor André Perold at the Harvard Business School. We started a case on tactical asset allocation intended for a course, but for various reasons, never completed it. Some sections of the case became Chapter 1 of this book.

After I joined J.P. Morgan Investment Management in 1996, I increased my understanding of several performance-related concepts while working with clients, consultants, and portfolio managers on various projects. When reviewing the practitioner literature on asset allocation, I found unproven assertions regarding asset allocation, and even found several myths. Moreover, very few of the articles I reviewed provided analytical rigor. I soon realized that an analytically rigorous work on asset allocation was needed.

One of the very first research questions I encountered was on the tactical trading rule. I was told a tactical trade could only be implemented when expected returns or premiums deviated from their equilibrium. Why did we underweight stocks against bonds for clients when our expected stock return was 8% and expected bond return was 6%? Would I do that with my own money? Could different objective functions lead to different trading rules, other than for reasons related to risk adjustment?

My attempt to answer these questions led me to review intertemporal and one-period portfolio theory. From what I had learned at graduate schools and with my newly acquired knowledge, I derived some useful results, which are presented in Chapter 2.

To the best of my knowledge, the information ratio is the most commonly used measure in evaluating asset allocation managers' performance. To my surprise, there appeared to be no standard approach to annualizing alphas and tracking errors. Often, I found the measures of different managers to be incompatible. Some simply annualize tracking error with the square root of time, without acknowledging that this is valid only when alphas are serially independent.

Without providing rigorous analysis, one asset allocation manager proposed that the hit ratio is a better measure of performance than the information ratio. I immediately disagreed. I interpreted the hit ratio as a measure of the frequency of success, and the information ratio as a measure of the consistency of profitability. Only in the special case when alpha is normally distributed would the two provide the same information. Instead of relying on the "best," I prefer to use a set of performance measures that provide different information. My thoughts on performance measures are presented in Chapter 3.

The impetus for Chapter 4 was my attempt to understand a widely used phrase, "volatility capture." Asset allocation managers claim that tactical asset allocation can add value only during volatile periods. Empirical evidence based on backtests and actual performance data seems to support this claim. My analysis suggested that there is indeed an analytical expression to characterize "volatility capture" as one component of alpha attributable to skills as well as volatilities. Volatility is a necessary but not sufficient condition for adding alphas.

Interestingly, I find a second component of alpha that has nothing to do with skills. This second component turns out to be related to the optimal trading rule in Chapter 2, and comes out of a debate I had with some colleagues: I suspected that simply overweighting the asset with the higher average return would increase the information ratio most of the time. I call this second component "alpha due to bias." I believe that many of my results in Chapter 4 are equally applicable to any active strategies attempting to outperform a static benchmark.

In one of my assignments, I was asked to help a group of macro strategists set forward-looking equilibrium to be used in tactical trading strategies — an extremely difficult project. Given the fact that I cannot tell what historical equilibrium is, even with a century of data and perfect hindsight, I doubted if I could set the forward-looking equilibrium. I took a short-cut and used backward-looking moving averages as proxies for equilibrium. To my surprise, this simple approach outperformed many variations of forward-looking equilibrium specifications. To better understand the properties of moving average strategies, I derived some expressions that characterize performance of these strategies. Furthermore, I found filtering the signals with moving averages an effective way of removing biases in models. These results are discussed in Chapter 5.

One consultant asked how trading ranges should be determined. Intuitively, how much we trade depends on the signals, attitudes toward risk, transaction costs, and some other constraints. I started to work on a robust framework to understand how optimal trading ranges should be determined, given the objective of maximizing the information ratio. Since futures contracts are used for tactical trades in asset allocation, I could drop transaction costs from my analysis. I call my derived framework *Optimal Aggressive Factors*.

The framework suggests that the aggressiveness of a particular trading strategy should be determined by its unique information advantage, what I call the "idiosyncratic information ratio." I also discovered a wide range of applications using the same framework, such as combining signals and strategies, and understanding how the number of signals and strategies, as well as a bias, affects the information ratio. Although derived differently, my framework confirms the "Fundamental Law of Active Management" in the highly regarding book on portfolio management by Richard Grinold and Ronald Kahn (*Active Portfolio Management*), but only under the stringent condition that the alphas of all trades are independent. These analyses are presented in Chapter 6.

Chapter 7 is based on my own notes on the Black-Litterman model. I find the application of Bayesian analysis in portfolio construction fascinating. Since the original articles, Black and Litterman (1991, 1992 — the references are provided in the Bibliography at the end of this book), do not show the details of their derivations, I had to work through some tedious matrix algebra myself. In doing so, I unveiled, through applications of some known results of Bayesian regressions, the intuition of combining views with equilibrium behind the matrix algebra. Although the Black-Litterman model is not designed to maximize the information ratio, it is a very useful portfolio construction tool, particularly for portfolios managed by strategists.

I hope that the reader finds the chapters in this book insightful in applications of asset allocation.

Wai Lee

Acknowledgments

I have a long list of people to thank. While I was writing my Ph.D. thesis and considering whether I would stay in academia or join a money management firm, I was fortunate to have joined the Division of Research at Harvard Business School. While I continued my studies by attending classes at Harvard University and the Massachusetts Institute of Technology, I also had the opportunity to work with Harvard professors on research, real industrial cases, and some consulting projects. This provided a perfect balance for me, which subsequently helped me decide to join the investment management industry.

I am indebted to Professor André Perold. In addition to being the best finance teacher I have ever had, in the two-year period I worked with him, he taught me aspects of finance that I could never learn from textbooks or research articles. André also provided me with invaluable comments, suggestions, and corrections on the first draft of this book.

Michael Granito hired me in the Capital Markets Research Group of J.P. Morgan Investment Management. I am fortunate to have worked with Mike, a unique and rare talent in the investment research industry. He taught me that elegant research can be applicable. Whenever there was a research problem that I could not solve, I knocked on Mike's door. Each time I left his office, I felt filled with ideas and answers. I am deeply grateful for his intellectual leadership.

Larry Smith, a boss, a mentor, a client, and a friend, has been a long-time supporter of my quantitative approach to investment management. Larry is one of the end-users of my research work. He filled me with challenges, ideas, questions, answers, and, of course, more work. I thank Larry for his inspiration, support, and care, and for providing a stimulating working environment.

I thank Timothy O'Hara for his careful review of my first draft and his many invaluable suggestions to make this book better. In fact, a large part of this book results from my response to many debates and discussions on asset allocation I had with him. With Tim, and from Tim, I learned asset allocation.

I thank Eric Remole, and members of the Global Structured Products Group at Credit Suisse Asset Management for their inspiration and support.

I have benefited from invaluable comments and suggestions from Jamil Baz, Campbell Harvey, and Antti Ilmanen.

I owe more debts than I can acknowledge, but I would like to thank some colleagues, clients, and friends for their advice and friendship: David Biberman, George Chacko, Ashvin Chhabra, Sanjiv Das, Christopher Durbin, James Gordon, Brian Johnson, Rhonda Kershner, Bernard Kroll, Thomas Luddy, Mehdi Mahmud, Brian Morris, Arun Muralidhar, Roberto Plaja, Marc Roston, Michael Schoenhaut, Stuart Schweitzer, C.S. Venkatakrishnan, Jian Yao, and Paul Zemsky.

I thank Frank Fabozzi for his encouragement and support throughout the preparation of this book. I am grateful for Patricia Peat for her patience and tolerance of my writing style.

And, finally, I owe more than I can say to the love and support of my family.

About the Author

Wai Lee is Director with the Global Structured Products Group of Credit Suisse Asset Management. He has published work on asset allocation, asset pricing, currency, interest rates, and quantitative methods in seven refereed financial economics journals, and contributed chapters to books on fixed-income securities. Abstracts of his research appear in *The CFA Digest*. He is an Advisory Board member of the *Journal of Portfolio Management*.

Prior to joining Credit Suisse Asset Management, Dr. Lee was the Head of Quantitative Research for the Global Balanced Group at J.P. Morgan Investment Management. Prior to joining J.P. Morgan, he was a Senior Research Associate in the Division of Research at Harvard Business School.

Dr. Lee has taught finance and economics at both the graduate and undergraduate level, and in executive management programs. He holds a B.Sc.(Hon.) degree in mechanical engineering from the University of Hong Kong, and M.B.A. and Ph.D. degrees in finance and quantitative methods from Drexel University, and has done postdoctoral work at Harvard University.

Chapter 1

Introduction

Tactical asset allocation (TAA) plays an important role in investment management.

The exact amount of investment engaged in TAA strategies is not clear. Philips, Rogers, and Capaldi (1996) estimate that as of the end of 1994, institutional investors had committed $48 billion to domestic TAA strategies. Since then and through April 2000, the S&P 500 and U.S. Treasury bonds had cumulative returns of about 250% and 60%, respectively. Assuming that the average holding is 50% stock, and 50% bonds, and that there was no new net cash flow into TAA strategies during this period, we can estimate that currently more than $120 billion is committed to TAA strategies. Although global TAA began only in the late 1980s, it has been growing much faster than domestic TAA because its broad scope and global nature fit very well with the globalization of investment.

Asset allocation policy is shown to be the overwhelmingly dominant factor in portfolio performance. Looking at return performance data from large pension plans, Brinson, Hood, and Beebower (1986) and Brinson, Singer, and Beebower (1991) find that, on average, asset allocation investment policy decisions explain more than 90% of the variation in quarterly total plan returns. Their results are further confirmed in a more recent study by Ibbotson and Kaplan (2000). When asset allocation decisions are tactically managed, overall portfolio performance will be significantly affected by the performance of TAA.

1.1 Historical Background

Wells Fargo is considered to be the first firm to introduce a tactical asset allocation product. After experiencing severe erosion of assets during the 1973-1974 market decline, some institutional investors began to search for asset allocation strategies that were better than ad hoc shifts among different asset classes. William Fouse of Wells Fargo Investment Advisors introduced a pioneer approach to implement asset allocation shifts between stocks and bonds. When the expected risk premium of stocks over bonds, according to dividends projected from current earnings estimates, was higher than a predetermined figure (about 3.5%), his system increased allocation to stocks from the normal mix, and vice versa. This system was able to produce positive results on paper between 1973 and 1976, a period of severe recession with a 45% stock market decline.

With the 27% market decline in 1981, TAA products began to gain popularity among institutional investors, and more managers started to launch similar systems in the investment industry.[1] When the use of derivatives took off in the 1980s, futures contracts were used to implement asset shifts, lowering the implementation cost of tactical asset shifts by as much as 90%.

Starting in the early 1980s, portfolio insurance, which was developed based on the option pricing theory of Black and Scholes (1973) and Merton (1973), was widely implemented by many institutional investors in attempt to produce a floor or guaranteed minimum portfolio return. This dynamic asset allocation strategy became even more popular when its implementation was greatly simplified by the introduction of Constant Proportion Portfolio Insurance (CPPI) by Perold (1986) and Black and Jones (1987). At around the same time, there was a major concern about TAA strategies as most of them had substantial hedges against stock when the stock market was rising.

The global market crash of October 1987 played an important role in shaping the future of TAA strategies and portfolio insurance. Before the crash, most valuation techniques viewed stock as significantly overvalued. However, the stock market continued to advance while bond yields were heading higher, leading to the first period of major underperformance for TAA managers. Since many TAA managers had substantially underweighted stock before the crash, and some were even hedged entirely out of stocks into bonds, these strategies did extremely well when stocks underperformed bonds by 30% in October 1987. About two weeks after the crash, many tactical managers restored their normal mix positions. Portfolio insurance strategies, however, largely failed to deliver a guaranteed floor value. Since then, there has been an explosive growth of interest in TAA strategies, while portfolio insurance has gradually faded away in the industry.

The Federal Funds rate was raised from 6.5% in April 1988 to 10.0% in March 1989. Most TAA strategies interpreted stock as relatively unattractive, causing substantial hedging of stock exposure from mid-1988 until mid-1989. Partly due to the gradual manner of the Federal Reserve's tight interest rate policy and its strong commitment to avoid a recession induced by high interest rates, together with corporate restructuring, leveraged buyouts, and foreign capital inflow, the stock market continued to rise strongly throughout the whole period of higher interest rates. This led to significant underperformance by many TAA managers. While those who had implemented TAA strategies prior to October 1987 still had a net positive incremental return, those who did so after the crash

---

[1] In an unpublished version of Philips, Rogers, and Capaldi (1996), it is reported that six managers had real-time tactical asset allocation performance dating back to 1982.

realized substantially lower returns than they would have without TAA.

After the recession in 1990, there was a secular decline of volatility of stock return in excess of bond. Since performance of TAA depends on volatility, it then became more and more difficult for TAA managers to add value for their clients.[2] Since 1995, volatility has appeared to return to more normal levels. In August 1998, stocks underperformed bonds by 20%. As volatility significantly bounced back, many TAA managers were said to have added value by underweighting stock.

Two decades of history suggest that returns of TAA strategies can be episodic. Unlike mutual funds, there is no formal performance evaluation measures for TAA managers. Some investment management consultants, such as BARRA RogersCasey and The Carmack Group, collect data from TAA managers. The Carmack Group currently tracks about two dozen TAA managers.

1.2 What Is Tactical Asset Allocation?

While TAA products have been around for more than two decades, a definition of TAA is not always clear. One of the problems is that the same terms are often applied to different strategies for different purposes. For instance, the term "dynamic asset allocation" is general enough to be used for any asset allocation strategies that change portfolio mix over time.[3] It can be used to describe tactical asset allocation, but it can be applied to portfolio insurance equally well. Since an option contract can be replicated by a dynamic trading rule, dynamic asset allocation is mostly used for portfolio insurance.

When TAA was first launched as an investment product, it was often marketed as a value-based investment strategy designed to realign the return and risk profile of the longer-term strategic benchmark portfolio. As a result, it gave the impression that a TAA strategy would buy cheap assets and sell expensive assets. The seminal study by Perold and Sharpe (1988) demonstrates that a constant-mix strategy requires purchase of assets as they fall in value, giving a concave payoff diagram. A portfolio insurance strategy would require purchase of assets as the price goes higher, thus giving a convex payoff diagram. After 1988, it became more popular to interpret TAA strategies as issuers/sellers of portfolio insurance. This interpretation was further strengthened by the fact that TAA managers had great performance during the crash of 1987, while portfolio insurers turned in poor performance.

The caveat about this interpretation is that not all TAA strategies would purchase stock when stock prices fall. For instance, managers who use momentum signals as part of their model are very likely to buy stocks when prices are going higher. Yet, we cannot say that they are not TAA managers.

---

[2] Merton (1981) is the first to link volatility to the performance of market timing strategies. Since then, the argument that high volatility is favorable for TAA strategies has been used at an intuitive level. See Philips, Rogers, and Capaldi (1996) and Arnott and Miller (1997), for example. The argument is formally proved in Lee (1998).

[3] For examples, see Arnott and Fabozzi (1988) and Trippi and Harriff (1991).

In Chapter 2, we discuss the theory behind normative and positive versions of TAA. Under the positive version in practice, TAA comes into play after strategic asset allocation decisions are made. In general, a benchmark portfolio is chosen on the basis of long-term equilibrium assumptions of return and risk of the investment universe, as well as the investor's attitude toward risk. However, current state can be driven further away or toward equilibrium by different market and economic forces such that the implicit optimal balance between return and risk in the strategic benchmark is off. It is thus necessary to change the portfolio compositions dynamically to restore optimality. Exactly how this is done depends on the information set or, in practical terms, the "tactical asset allocation" model.

Arnott and Fabozzi (1988, p. 4) define TAA this way:

> Tactical asset allocation broadly refers to active strategies which seek to enhance performance by opportunistically shifting the asset mix of a portfolio in response to the changing patterns of reward available in the capital markets. Notably, tactical asset allocation tends to refer to disciplined processes for evaluating prospective rates of return on various asset classes and establishing an asset allocation response intended to capture higher rewards. In the various implementations of tactical asset allocation, there are different investment horizons and different mechanisms for evaluating the asset allocation decision.

This is indeed a very broad definition. It covers most, if not all, tactical asset allocation strategies, but it never clearly defines what "to enhance performance" and "rewards" really mean. Therefore, whether a particular strategy is a TAA strategy or not depends on how performance and rewards are measured, whether in terms of return, volatility, Sharpe ratio, or mean-variance efficiency, and the like.

Philips, Rogers, and Capaldi (1996) put forth a more practical definition for TAA:

> A TAA manager's investment objective is to obtain better-than-benchmark returns with (possibly) lower-than-benchmark volatility by forecasting the returns of two or more asset classes, and varying asset class exposure accordingly, in a *systematic* manner.

In practice, performance of TAA managers is always measured against their passive benchmark portfolios. If the manager outperforms the benchmark so that the return of the TAA portfolio is higher than the return of the benchmark portfolio, the manager is said to have delivered a positive "alpha." Consistency of outperformance is also important. Generally speaking, a manager who is able to deliver more consistent outperformance, commonly measured by the volatility of alpha (known as the "tracking error"), is considered to be more skillful. Like the Sharpe ratio, which takes both return and risk into account, one typical measure for comparing performance of different TAA managers is the information ratio, defined as the ratio of alpha to tracking error. The higher the information ratio, the better.

One may argue that the way Philips, Rogers, and Capaldi define TAA seems to overemphasize return and understate the importance of risk. Nor may outperformance of the benchmark be consistent with maximizing mean-variance efficiency of the portfolio, as the TAA manager may deliver a better-than-benchmark return at the cost of a higher-than-benchmark volatility.

It is fair to point out that the return and risk trade-off, or the mean-variance efficiency of the overall portfolio, is an important metric to evaluate performance. In practice, however, a TAA manager who consistently delivers negative alphas even if improving overall mean-variance efficiency will certainly go out of business. This is partly because most clients of TAA managers are institutional investors who have long enough investment horizon that some additional volatility is not unacceptable. Moreover, measuring a portfolio's mean-variance efficiency remains an extremely difficult task.[4] The extent of measurement error needs to be mitigated before mean-variance efficiency can become a more important tool for portfolio performance measurement.

In this book, we use a simple definition for TAA strategy:

"TAA strategies are strategies that attempt to deliver a positive information ratio by systematic asset allocation shifts."

1.3   Implementing Tactical Asset Allocation

In practice, TAA is frequently offered as an overlay program to the underlying equity fund and bond fund. Consider a 50/50 stock/bond benchmark portfolio, 20% of which is committed to a TAA program. The participant typically chooses the normal mix, 50/50 in this example, with the help of the investment manager. With $100 million total assets, $50 million would be allocated to equities and $50 million to bonds. $10 million is then contributed from each fund to the 20% TAA program. If the manager is bullish on stocks and bearish on bonds, Treasury bond futures equivalent to part or all of the $10 million in bonds in the TAA program could be sold, and the proceeds used to purchase S&P futures, thus increasing exposure to stocks. The reverse happens for bearish on stocks and bullish on bonds. If the manager is bearish on both stocks and bonds, S&P futures and Treasury bond futures would be sold to gain cash exposure. This structure allows a maximum exposure of 60%, 60%, and 20% and a minimum exposure of 40%, 40%, and 0% to equities, bonds, and cash, respectively. Thus, the normal mix portfolio becomes the benchmark in calculating the value added by the TAA program.

TAA programs can be run even when some asset classes are not in the underlying portfolio. Suppose an underlying physical portfolio is 100% stock, while the benchmark portfolio is chosen as 60% in stocks and 40% in bonds.

---

[4] See Shanken (1987) and Gibbons, Ross, and Shanken (1989) for tests of portfolio efficiency. Britten-Jones (1999) illustrates the large sampling error in estimates of mean-variance efficient portfolio weights.

Instead of selling physical stocks in an amount equal to 40% of the portfolio and buying bonds with the proceeds, the appropriate number of S&P futures contracts can be sold and the proceeds used to buy Treasury bond futures to bring the exposures to stocks and bonds to the desired benchmark levels of 60% and 40%. Futures contracts for tactical shifts can then be traded. Similarly, a domestic portfolio with no exposure to foreign assets can also be used to run global TAA; the appropriate number of futures contracts for domestic assets may be sold to raise the amount necessary to buy futures contracts for foreign assets.

1.4   Organization of the Book

The core of this book consists of three parts. Chapter 2, which offers a purely portfolio theory perspective in explaining the role and importance of TAA, constitutes Part I. Most of the work on TAA is written from an empirical perspective, or as marketing materials of investment managers.[5] Chapter 2 attempts to offer an objective view of the normative aspects of implementing TAA strategies within the fundamental framework of analysis in modern finance theory: the maximizing of expected utility over time. The theoretical approach assumes that a rational risk-averse investor will hold risky assets not only because of the compensation of their risk premium, but also for hedging future unfavorable investment conditions. However, this approach is far too complex for today's computing technology to handle, so it remains largely normative in nature. Accordingly, the second part of Chapter 2 takes a positive standpoint to analyze TAA in practice using a one-period model. Perspectives based on total risk and total return versus active risk and active return are compared.

Chapters 3, 4, and 5 make up Part II, which deals with various performance issues. Chapter 3 covers some of the most commonly used performance measures for TAA managers, including alpha, tracking error, information ratio, hit ratio, and Henriksson-Merton and Cumby-Modest tests. It also discusses a variety of issues related to annualizing performance measures and relationships among performance measures.

Chapter 4 is an expanded version of Lee (1998). Instead of analyzing performance characteristics based on live performance data of TAA managers or simulation, it uses some general assumptions to derive analytically tractable expressions for performance measures under uncertainty.[6] Since only a few basic assumptions are made in the derivation, the results are general enough to

---

[5] The empirical work includes Breen, Glosten, and Jagannathan (1989), Clarke, FitzGerald, Berent, and Statman (1989, 1990), Sy (1990), Weigel (1991), Shilling (1992), Wagner, Shellans, and Paul (1992), Chen, Chan, and Mohan (1993), MacBeth and Emanuel (1993), Boudoukh (1994), Brocato and Chandy (1994), Nam and Branch (1994), Philips, Rogers, and Capaldi (1996), Vergin (1996), Brennan, Schwartz, and Lagnado (1997), Lee (1997d), and Wagner (1997).

[6] For performance analysis, see Philips, Rogers, and Capaldi (1996), for example. For simulations, see Weigel (1991), Brennan, Schwartz, and Lagnado (1997), and Lee (1997d), among others.

be used as first-order approximations for all TAA strategies. We use the results to discuss how a bias in favor of the higher return asset may affect the overall information ratio, as well as to draw realistic expectations on performance of TAA strategies. Although higher-moments evaluation criteria, such as skewness, are outside the scope of this book, Chapter 4 also sheds light on the fact that successful TAA strategies induce positive skewness in portfolio returns distributions.

Building upon the analysis of bias in Chapter 4, Chapter 5 discusses a methodology for mitigating bias in tactical trading rules through signal filtering. As in Chapter 4, all results in Chapter 5 are derived according to some basic assumptions on the dynamics of signals and returns. The pros and cons of signal filtering are discussed in detail.

Part III, which includes Chapters 6, 7, and 8, deals with portfolio construction. In practice, almost all TAA strategies are run with multiple signals and multiple pairwise bets on a set of assets. Chapter 6 derives the optimal aggressiveness factor framework by which to achieve the maximum overall information ratio of the final TAA portfolio, given expectations of alphas and covariance matrix among different signals and bets. Five case studies are presented to illustrate the broad scope of application of the framework. For example, the framework can be used to analyze the marginal contribution of each signal or bet to the overall information ratio. The results have important implications for issues such as the effect of convergence in Europe on overall performance of a global TAA portfolio, as well as how a structural bet may increase or decrease the overall information ratio.

Chapter 7 articulates a totally different portfolio construction approach pioneered by Black and Litterman (1991, 1992). The original Black-Litterman model is designed to combine relative views of assets with equilibrium according to a Bayesian framework. Besides elaborating the conceptual underpinnings and technical details of the model, we discuss how the model can be applied for TAA portfolios. Finally, Chapter 8 is an epilogue on some experience of portfolio construction for TAA.

Although this book is about TAA, we believe that many of the results as well as the approach and the framework of analysis can be applied to other active investment products, as long as the objective is to add value, given views or forecasts of relative values. The major difference is that transaction costs can largely be ignored because of the low cost of trading futures contracts in TAA. This assumption is valid for products such as tactical duration management, and tactical currency management, as long as liquid futures contracts are available. In active equity portfolio management, transaction costs should be explicitly considered.

Chapter 2

Tactical Asset Allocation: A Portfolio Theory Perspective

2.1 Introduction

Why should asset allocation be tactically managed?

One of the few seminal studies in putting asset allocation decisions into a presentable framework is Sharpe (1987). Implicitly based on a one-period model, Sharpe argues that, given the same investment opportunity set, investors with different attitude toward risk will have different responses to asset allocation decisions.[1] Sharpe compares and contrasts strategic asset allocation, tactical asset allocation (TAA), and portfolio insurance strategies. An investor will stay with a constant-mix strategic portfolio, provided that *relative* risk tolerance does not change and expected returns, risks, and correlations are all believed to be constant. When the investor attempts to predict expected returns and covariance matrix, or when these parameters are believed to be time-varying, however, the investor will choose tactical asset allocation. Constant *relative* risk tolerance is the condition in common in both strategic and tactical asset allocation strategies.

An investor with the same attitude toward risk will be more willing to buy risky assets when risk is expected to be high or when the price of the asset is depressed. Largely due to Sharpe's work, some tactical asset allocation managers argue that it is because of this level of discomfort that tactical asset allocation is rewarded.

---

[1] Throughout this book, "investment opportunity set" stands for the return distributions of all assets, which can be time-varying. In a standard mean-variance framework, the investment opportunity set can be specified by the vector of expected returns and the covariance matrix of all assets.

Finally, Sharpe shows that an investor whose relative risk tolerance increases with wealth will choose to implement portfolio insurance. As wealth increases, the investor has higher risk tolerance, which in turn leads to increasing portfolio positions in risky assets. Similarly, when wealth decreases, the investor becomes more risk-averse, thus increasing holdings of the risk-free asset.

Clarke (1997) suggests that a tactical asset allocation portfolio can be treated as a stand-alone asset class with its own risk and return characteristics. Provided that one agrees with this view, implementing a tactical asset allocation strategy clearly enhances portfolio efficiency as it simply becomes a diversification tool for the overall portfolio. In this way, the efficient frontier based on long-term expected returns and covariance matrix is expanded.

A potential caveat with regard to this approach is that a tactical asset allocation portfolio is itself a portfolio of other assets in the benchmark portfolio, which are used to generate the efficient frontier. It is not immediately clear why a portfolio of the same asset universe should be viewed as a stand-alone "asset class" within the same universe. The whole argument may bring us to the issue of one-period versus multi-period analysis, as the weights in the tactical asset allocation portfolio are not fixed over time, unlike any other stand-alone assets within the portfolio frontier.

While its focus is not on investment products, a study by Kandel and Stambaugh (1996) offers interesting insights into the economic significance of time-varying investment opportunity sets for asset allocation decisions. Kandel and Stambaugh attempt to understand how an investor may use predictability of returns to adjust portfolio holdings over time.

It is well documented that monthly returns are difficult to predict, although there is evidence that they are predictable. Empirical evidence suggests that R-squares of regressing monthly returns on sets of predicting variables typically range from zero to a few percent, and an R-square of 10% is truly exceptional. For example, in regressing the real value-weighted NYSE stock return on the lagged return, dividend-price ratio, and the one-month T-bill rate minus its past twelve-month moving average, Campbell (1991) reports an R-square of only 2.4%.

With such a low degree of predictability and therefore uncertainty of future returns remains high, it is hard to see that the predictability of returns for the investor's asset allocation decisions can be economically significant. Kandel and Stambaugh, however, demonstrate that using these results to update the investor's prior beliefs on the probability distribution of future returns has a significant impact on current asset allocation decisions. Their analysis suggests that evidence on predictability of returns can be sufficient to have an economically significant impact on asset allocations, even though a null hypothesis of no predictability might not be rejected at conventional levels of statistical significance.

There are several schools of thought on predictability of returns. Campbell, Lo, and MacKinlay (1997) and Lo (1997) provide good coverage of the topic, and a full discussion would be beyond the scope of this book. Putting the literature on returns predictability together with Kandel and Stambaugh's results, though, explains why investors continue to make tactical decisions on portfolio composition.

On the other hand, evidence against the predictability of returns is often used to make a case against implementing TAA. Bossaerts and Hillion (1999) apply formal statistical model selection criteria to determine the best linear regression model with varying numbers of predictors to predict excess stock returns in an international data set. They conclude that the evidence of stock return predictability documented is not due to model overfitting. While they also find that even the best model cannot be validated in out-of-sample tests, they are careful enough to point out that their findings demonstrate only nonstationarity in linear models of stock returns.

It is premature to draw the conclusion that no model will work in predicting stock returns. Instead, the evidence seems to suggest that linear regression models should be revised constantly. In addition, the effectiveness of nonlinear models is not covered in Bossaerts and Hillion.

Unlike most other studies and unlike the marketing materials of investment managers, which typically use live or simulated performance, this chapter provides a purely theoretical justification for tactical asset allocation based on a portfolio theory perspective. We argue that the theoretically optimal tactical asset allocation strategy is supported in Merton's (1973, 1990) solution to the intertemporal consumption and portfolio decision problem. With a changing investment opportunity set, a risk-averse investor will hold risky assets not only for the positive risk premium and diversification, but also for intertemporal hedging. Unfortunately, the complexity and dimension of the problem makes realistic applications of the multi-period framework practically impossible.

We introduce the standard practice in investment management, the simple one-period portfolio optimization approach, to show that tactical asset allocation is inherently important in maximizing expected utility. Acknowledge that the resulting trading rule can be suboptimal, as it ignores the intertemporal hedging component, we further elaborate the different components in the optimal portfolio weights, and explain the pairwise bet structure embedded in the solution. Both total return/total risk and active return/active risk perspectives will be compared and contrasted.

2.2 Tactical Asset Allocation in Theory: Multi-Period Intertemporal Analysis

Realistically, portfolio and consumption choice should be analyzed in a multi-period setting. Unfortunately, the problem easily becomes far more complicated and less tractable. Even with the power of continuous-time mathematics, explicit solutions for optimal portfolio composition are available only in those few special cases in which the multi-period problem can be reduced to a simple one-period problem such that the investor follows a myopic portfolio strategy as if it were a one-period problem.

Samuelson (1969) and Merton (1969, 1971, 1973, 1990) have shown that optimal portfolio strategies are significantly affected by the stochastic investment opportunity set. By now, few would disagree that expected returns, and possibly variances and covariances, are time-varying and to some extent, predictable.[2] As a result, it is essential to understand the problem from a multi-period perspective in order to appreciate the role of tactical asset allocation. However, because of its degree of complexity, we use only the important results in the subject to illustrate our points. No proofs or derivations are given. Readers should consult standard references on multi-period portfolio decision making.[3]

We follow the intertemporal capital asset pricing framework of Merton (1973). We demonstrate that in an intertemporal setting with multiple periods in the investment horizon, there are two components in the optimal allocation to a particular asset: a myopic component depending on the expected risk premium, and an intertemporal hedging component to hedge against the stochastic investment opportunity set.

Once the framework is laid out, we explain why this theoretically optimal intertemporal framework for tactical asset allocation cannot yet be implemented. This leads us to one-period analysis, which is the standard for tactical asset allocation managers in practice.

2.2.1   Multi-Period Portfolio and Consumption Choice

Suppose there is one "risk-free" asset with a constant rate of return r, and n assets in the investment universe, labelled as $i = 1, 2, ..., n$, with expected returns and covariance matrix given by the vector $E[\mathbf{R}]$ and the matrix Ω, respectively. That is, the i-th element of $E[\mathbf{R}]$ denotes the expected return of asset i, and the ij-th element of Ω denotes the covariance of returns of asset i and asset j. The information in $E[\mathbf{R}]$ and Ω defines what we call the investment opportunity set.[4]

To simplify, we assume that a finite-horizon investor is faced with the problem of deciding the level of consumption today, C_t. The savings is then allocated to the risk-free asset and a portfolio of risky assets with the vector of one-period returns denoted by $\widetilde{\mathbf{R}}_{t+1}$, where $\sim$ denotes that the variable is stochastic. For simplicity, we assume that the risk-free rate of return is constant. In each period t, the investor consumes a fraction of wealth, W_t, and invests the savings in the risk-free asset and the portfolio of risky assets. The vector of portfolio weights, ω, has n elements as the weights in the n risky assets. As a result, $(1 - \omega'\mathbf{1})$ denotes the portfolio weight of the risk-free asset.

To characterize the investor's preference by means of a utility function, we assume that the objective of the investor is to maximize the expected utility

---

[2] An excellent collection of articles on market efficiency is Lo (1997), and the references cited there as well.

[3] Standard references include Campbell, Lo, and MacKinlay (1997), Duffie (1996), Dothan (1990), Merton (1990), and Ingersoll (1987).

[4] Strictly speaking, we also need to specify how $E[\mathbf{R}]$ and Ω change over time, which we discuss later when we introduce state variables.

of lifetime consumption, which is further assumed to be time separable and additive. Therefore, the problem can be specified as

$$\max_{C_t,\omega_t} E\left[U\left(C_t, C_{t+1}, ..., C_T\right)\right] = \max_{\{c_\tau,\omega_\tau\}_{\tau=t}^T} E\left[\sum_{\tau=t}^T \beta^{\tau-t} U\left(C_\tau\right)\right] \qquad (2.1)$$

subject to $\widetilde{W}_{t+1} = (W_t - C_t)\left[(1 - \omega_t'\mathbf{1})\,r + \omega_t'\widetilde{\mathbf{R}}_{t+1}\right]$

where $\beta < 1$ is a discount factor for computing present values. It can be interpreted as a measure of willingness to give up consumption this period for consumption next period.

This problem can be solved by the stochastic dynamic programming technique by defining the value function J given by the Bellman equation:[5]

$$J\left(W_t, T - t\right) = \max_{C_t,\omega_t} U\left(C_t\right) + \beta E\left[J\left(\widetilde{W}_{t+1}, T - t - 1\right)\right] \qquad (2.2)$$

In the asset pricing literature, the most commonly used utility function is the class which exhibits constant relative risk aversion. For example:

$$U\left(C_t\right) = \begin{cases} \frac{C_t^{1-\kappa}}{1-\kappa} & \text{for } \kappa > 0 \text{ and } \kappa \neq 1; \\ \ln\left(C_t\right) & \text{for } \kappa = 0 \end{cases} \qquad (2.3)$$

The power utility function is one of the most widely applied functions. We will illustrate that under the logarithmic utility function, the multi-period problem will collapse to a one-period problem. In this case, the investor is said to be myopic, as the optimal portfolio strategy is identical to the solution of the one-period problem such that the problem is solved as if the investment horizon were only one period. To simplify the analysis, some prefer to use a utility function defined on the terminal wealth only, assuming that there is no intermediate consumption withdrawal.

To simplify the notation, we drop the time subscript t from here on. In a first-order condition, it can be shown that the marginal utility of wealth, denoted as the first derivative of J with respect to W, J_W, is equal to the marginal utility of current consumption, which is denoted as the first derivative of U with respect to C, U_C. That is:

$$\frac{\partial J}{\partial W} = \frac{\partial U}{\partial C} \qquad (2.4)$$

As a result, J is also known as the indirect utility function.

From the Bellman equation (2.2), the level of utility this period clearly depends on the level of wealth next period, which in turn is determined by the

---

[5] See Merton (1990) for details. The problem can also be solved by the martingale method of Cox and Huang (1989), applied in Duffie (1996), for example.

portfolio and consumption choices to be made today, as well as the future investment opportunity set that will subsequently affect the future portfolio and consumption decisions. Therefore, the problem has to be solved recursively. It is this recursive nature of the solution that makes today's portfolio and consumption decisions dependent on the investor's expectations of the future. In other words, the investor is no longer myopic.

Unless some very specific conditions to be discussed later are satisfied so that a multi-period problem can be reduced to a one-period problem, the optimal portfolio choice varies at a minimum with time, with the investment opportunity set, and with the degree of risk aversion. Only in the final period of the multi-period setting will the myopic and nonmyopic portfolios be identical, when both have a one-period investment horizon.

To introduce a stochastic investment opportunity set in the simplest setting, suppose there is a single state variable, x, such that at least one parameter of the return distributions of the risky assets is correlated with x.[6] In other words, the investment opportunity set is driven by the dynamics of x.

For example, expected returns of the risky assets may depend on inflation. In this case, the parameters of the return distributions are the expected returns, while the inflation rate is the single state variable.[7] Or, the return distribution parameter can be the covariance matrix as well such that volatilities and correlations can change with inflation.[8]

Solving equation (2.2) with the technique of stochastic dynamic programming, we obtain the vector of optimal portfolio weights as

$$\omega^* = A\mathbf{M} + B\mathbf{H} \tag{2.5}$$

where

$$A = -\frac{J_W}{W J_{WW}} = -\frac{U_C}{W U_{CC} \left(\frac{\partial C}{\partial W}\right)} > 0 \tag{2.6}$$

$$B = -\frac{J_{xW}}{W J_{WW}} = -\frac{-\frac{\partial C}{\partial x}}{W \frac{\partial C}{\partial W}} \lessgtr 0 \tag{2.7}$$

$$\mathbf{M} = \Omega^{-1}\left(E\left[\mathbf{R}\right] - r\mathbf{1}\right) \tag{2.8}$$

$$\mathbf{H} = \Omega^{-1}\boldsymbol{\nu} \tag{2.9}$$

---

[6] A more general case will involve any number of state variables that describe the economy and investment opportunity set. The solution technique as well as implications are simular to the case with a single state variable.

[7] For empirical evidence on stock return and inflation, see Breen, Glosten, and Jagannathan (1989), Fama (1981), Fama and Schwert (1977), Froot (1990), Geske and Roll (1983), Kaul (1987, 1990), Lee (1997d), and Solnik (1983).

[8] See Erb, Harvey, and Viskanta (1994) for an analysis of global business cycles, inflations, and correlations among equity markets.

and

$$\nu' = (\sigma_{1x}, \sigma_{2x}, ..., \sigma_{nx}) \tag{2.10}$$

The variable A is proportional to the investor's relative risk tolerance, while B is a measure of the investor's aversion to changes in the state variable x. Each element in the vector ν denotes the covariance of each asset with changes in the state variable.[9]

2.2.2 Myopic and Intertemporal Hedging Components

The solution to the Bellman equation suggests that, in general, there are two components in the investor's allocation to the risky assets, AM and BH. The *myopic* component, denoted as AM, is the demand of the risky asset due to its risk premium, and is directly proportional to the investor's risk tolerance. It has been shown that this component is the same as the solution to a one-period mean-variance maximizer.[10] Because of this, it earns the name *myopic*, as it is optimal only if the investor looks no further than this period.

Under realistic parameters, this component is positive, suggesting that a typical investor will hold some risky assets. It can be shown that this component can be reexpressed as a direct function of the tangency portfolio of the standard efficient frontier and the borrowing-lending straight line from the risk-free asset.[11] Therefore, this myopic component provides the optimal diversification, given the investment opportunity set available to the investor.

The *intertemporal hedging* component, denoted as BH, represents the desire to hedge against future adverse changes in the investment opportunity set driven by the state variable x. The exact functional form of this component can vary substantially with specification of the utility function as well as how the investor uses the information set to form expectations of the future investment opportunity set.

Generally speaking, a change in the investment opportunity set is unfavorable if, for a given level of future wealth, future consumption will fall when x changes. Mathematically, an increase in x is an unfavorable change if $\partial C/\partial x < 0$; that is, an increase in x leads to a decrease in future consumption and thus a lower level of utility.

It can be shown that the hedging component is the portfolio of risky assets that has the maximum possible absolute correlation with the state variable.[12] This means that, for example, when there is an unfavorable change in the opportunity set (x increases in our example) such that future consumption is going to be lower, a risk-averse utility maximizer will demand more of the assets that have positive correlations with x. These assets tend to have higher returns when

---

[9]Relative risk aversion is defined as $-U''(C)C/U'(C)$; relative risk tolerance is just the inverse of the relative risk aversion.

[10]See Merton (1972).

[11]See Ingersoll (1987) for details.

[12]See Ingersoll (1987) and Merton (1990) for details.

x increases, which will be more valuable when consumption level is low. Therefore, the hedging component provides the optimal hedge against unfavorable changes in the state variable through intertemporal consumption smoothing.

We can use some simple examples to illustrate the point. Suppose the equilibrium return of the risky asset is 10%, and the realized return in the most recent period is 0%. Having read some of the research findings on mean reversion in asset prices, the investor believes that the return of the risky asset is negatively autocorrelated.[13] Since realized return is low, expected future returns should be high. Therefore, the investor forms an expected conditional probability distribution of future risky asset returns. For example, the expected return of the risky asset is 15% next period.

Because the investor expects a higher risk premium in the future, the decision is to increase the portfolio allocation to the risky asset today. Conversely, the allocation to the risky asset may be reduced if the most recent period's realized return is, say, 20%.

Therefore, a fixed-weight portfolio strategy, such as a 70/30 portfolio in risky asset/risk-free asset, can be interpreted as a suboptimal strategy when mean reversion is taken into account. The strategy is suboptimal in that it is not appropriately calibrated so that the investor will respond differently to different realized returns. Yet this type of constant-mix strategy is widely recommended by consultants, and discussed in some detail in Perold and Sharpe (1988) and Siegel (1998).

As an example of how intertemporal hedging can change optimal holdings of risky assets, consider a simple two-period world in which there are only three risky assets: stock, a one-period bond, and a two-period bond.[14] Further assume that the pure expectations hypothesis holds such that the expected returns of the one-period and two-period bonds are exactly the same. In this case, a myopic risk-averse utility maximizer, who cares only about the risk premium, will not hold any two-period bond because its return is subject to the risk of changes in interest rates and it does not offer any risk premium over the one-period bond.

On the other hand, a nonmyopic investor who behaves optimally will realize that this risky two-period bond, even though its expected return is the same as the one-period bond, may be used to hedge against future unfavorable conditions. For instance, if bond yield goes up in the first period such that the two-period bond has a lower return than the one-period bond, it will be compensated for by the higher reinvestment rate from the end of the first period to the second period.

In this simple example, the optimal portfolios of the myopic investor and the nonmyopic investor with a long-term horizon will clearly be different. The former will invest in a particular asset if and only if it offers a positive risk premium (myopic component only, AM), while the latter will also consider the asset as a hedge against the changing investment opportunity set, in additional to its risk premium (myopic and intertemporal components, AM + BH).

---

[13] See, for example, Fama and French (1988).
[14] This example is taken from Brennan, Schwartz, and Lagnado (1997).

2.2.3   Optimal Tactical Asset Allocation Rule

Equation (2.5) shows how asset allocation should be tactically managed through time, provided that the objective is to maximize a prespecified utility function. According to equation (2.5), optimal tactical allocation to assets should change over time if any terms or parameters in the equation change. Possible scenarios can be grouped into two categories: changes in preferences and wealth and changes in investment opportunity set.

Changes in Preferences and Wealth

A and B are functions of measures of risk tolerance, aversion to unfavorable changes in state variables, and the level of wealth. They will assume different values if attitude toward risk changes. In reality, investors have different degrees of risk tolerance. For the same investor, it is also possible that attitude toward risk may change with age, or experience, or level of wealth, and the like.[15]

In general, the relative proportions of the assets held by the investor in the optimal portfolio are not independent of preferences. This makes understanding tactical asset allocation due to changes in preferences and wealth difficult.

We can articulate using some additional matrix algebra and redefined terms. Rewrite equation (2.5) as

$$\omega^* = A^\dagger \mathbf{M}^\dagger + B^\dagger \mathbf{H}^\dagger \qquad (2.11)$$

where

$$A^\dagger = -\frac{J_W}{W J_{WW}} \mathbf{1}' \Omega^{-1} \left(E\left[\mathbf{R}\right] - r\mathbf{1} \right) \qquad (2.12)$$

$$B^\dagger = -\frac{J_{xW}}{W J_{WW}} \mathbf{1}' \Omega^{-1} \nu \qquad (2.13)$$

$$\mathbf{M}^\dagger = \frac{\Omega^{-1} \left(E\left[\mathbf{R}\right] - r\mathbf{1} \right)}{\mathbf{1}' \Omega^{-1} \left(E\left[\mathbf{R}\right] - r\mathbf{1} \right)} \qquad (2.14)$$

and

$$\mathbf{H}^\dagger = \frac{\Omega^{-1} \nu}{\mathbf{1}' \Omega^{-1} \nu} \qquad (2.15)$$

In addition, it is easy to verify that

$$\mathbf{1}' \mathbf{M}^\dagger = \mathbf{1}' \mathbf{H}^\dagger = 1 \qquad (2.16)$$

---

[15] The finance literature often assumes utility functions with constant relative risk aversion (CRRA), which also gives rise to constant relative risk tolerance independent of wealth. Recent studies, such as Sharpe (1990), argue that when wealth is relatively low, investors become more risk averse and demand a higher compensation for risk. Campbell and Cochrane (1999) derive a model with countercyclic varying risk aversion due to the force of habit in past consumption.

such that $\mathbf{M}^\dagger$ and $\mathbf{H}^\dagger$ are now vectors of weights for two distinct portfolios of risky assets in the same investment universe. More important, the relative proportions of assets in these two portfolios are now independent of preferences and wealth, becoming functions of the investment opportunity set only. It can thus be seen that the optimal portfolio for each investor consists of different positions in these two portfolios, and the positions depend on the values of $A^\dagger$ and $B^\dagger$ of the investor. Given the same investment opportunity set, the optimal portfolio for each investor will be tactically managed in accordance with how $A^\dagger$ and $B^\dagger$ change.

In fact, it is easy to show that the portfolio $\mathbf{M}^\dagger$ is indeed the tangency portfolio of the efficient portfolio frontier of risky assets and the risk-free borrowing-lending straight line, while the portfolio $\mathbf{H}^\dagger$ preserves the property that it has the maximum absolute correlation with the state variable. In other words, these two portfolios provide optimal diversification and an optimal hedge against changes in the investment opportunity set.

For example, every thing else equal, if the investor is becoming more risk-tolerant with respect to variance risk (i.e., $-J_W/J_{WW}W$ increases), more weight will be put in the portfolio $\mathbf{M}^\dagger$. Similarly, if the investor is becoming more risk-tolerant with respect to the risk of changing investment opportunity (i.e., $-J_{xW}/J_{WW}W$ increases), more weight will be put in the portfolio $\mathbf{H}^\dagger$.

Changes in Investment Opportunity Set

According to equation (2.5), the optimal allocation to risky assets should change in accordance with the investment opportunity set that is captured by the vectors $\mathbf{M}$ and $\mathbf{H}$. As the state variables change, the investor will reallocate positions with respect to the return distribution parameters. For instance, expected returns are functions of some state variables including interest rate and dividend yield.[16] As these state variables change, so do the expected returns. Consequently, allocations to risky assets will be changed in accordance with the new expected risk premiums.

Alternatively, the covariance matrix, Ω, or the covariances of assets with the state variables, ν, can change with the state variables.[17] In this case, even if there is no change in expected risk premium, the risk profile of the assets and the hedging demand have changed, so the optimal allocation to assets will be different.

2.2.4 Solving the Optimal Tactical Asset Allocation Rule

Implementing the optimal tactical asset allocation rule requires solving a highly nonlinear partial differential equation of utility, J. The solution to the problem

---

[16] See the empirical evidence in Fama and French (1989).

[17] There are relatively few studies that focus on how changes in the covariance matrix affect optimal portfolio decisions. Some examples include Chacko and Viceira (1999), and Kim and Omberg (1996).

is a dynamic consumption and portfolio strategy contingent on the level of current wealth and state variables. Unfortunately, because of the nonlinearity and the potentially high number of state variables in the system, there is generally no closed-form solution available except for some very special cases.[18]

In realistic cases, the differential equation has to be solved numerically with some finite difference approximation. Complexity grows geometrically with the number of assets and state variables. Our current computing power allows the solving of only some highly simplified problems with a limited number of assets and state variables. Therefore, *the optimal tactical asset allocation remains largely theoretical.*

Brennan, Schwartz, and Lagnado (1997) solve the optimal portfolio problem when returns are predictable. The authors assume that an investor can invest in stocks, bonds, and cash. Time-varying expected returns of these assets are driven by some state variables, which include the short-term interest rate, the long-term interest rate, and dividend yield. The optimal control problem is then solved numerically, and implications for asset allocation decisions as a function of the investment horizon are drawn accordingly.

The results suggest that when returns are predictable, the optimal portfolio held by a nonmyopic investor with a longer investment horizon is sufficiently different from the optimal portfolio held by a myopic investor. Simulation results confirm that returns predictability is sufficient for tactical strategies to yield significant improvements in portfolio performance.

Barberis (2000) also solves the problem numerically. On the other hand, Campbell and Viceira (1999) derive approximate analytical solution by imposing additional assumptions on the utility function and the dynamics of the real interest rate and state variables. Related studies include Campbell, Cocco, Gomes, Maenhout, and Viceira (1998) and Brandt (1999), among many others.

2.2.5   What Is TAA Again?

The basics of intertemporal portfolio theory should allow one to appreciate the broad scope of TAA as depicted by equation (2.5). This equation is the solution to the dynamic portfolio optimization problem in which the investor specifies the preference function and the evolution over time of the stochastic investment opportunity set. Provided that explicit solution under some specific conditions to be discussed in the next section is available, or that a numerical solution is feasible, implementing equation (2.5) is the unique solution maximizing the investor's objective function.

If one interprets "enhance performance" as to increase the value of the objective function, the definition of TAA put forth by Arnott and Fabozzi (1988, p. 4) as mentioned in Chapter 1 is in fact consistent with the normative, intertemporal analysis of TAA. A potential drawback of this definition is that,

---

[18]See Merton (1990), Chapter 5. An approximate analytical solution is possible with additional assumptions on utility function and dynamics of state variables; see Campbell and Viceira (1999).

by picking a particular class of utility function, one may even put portfolio insurance strategies under this broad definition. This may create confusion, as the investment industry seems to have an unambiguous understanding of what portfolio insurance strategies are.[19]

2.2.6   Equivalence of Intertemporal and Myopic Strategies

It is useful to investigate under what conditions the optimal intertemporal portfolio trading rule will collapse to the optimal trading rule derived from a one-period setting. In this case, we could still argue that there is no loss of efficiency or welfare measured by utility in implementing tactical asset allocation as if it were a myopic strategy.

The main difference between the optimal portfolio rule of a myopic investor with a one-period horizon and a nonmyopic investor with a longer horizon is the intertemporal hedging component in equation (2.5). While both types of investors will hold risky assets for their positive risk premium, the nonmyopic investor will also consider holding more or less of the risky assets for hedging purposes. Therefore, the portfolio strategies become identical when the intertemporal hedging component is zero.

There are generally two conditions under which the intertemporal hedging component term in equation (2.5) is zero: in the presence of a nonstochastic investment opportunity set, or a logarithmic utility function.[20]

Nonstochastic Investment Opportunity Set

Obviously, the intertemporal hedging component will become zero when there is nothing to hedge. Consider the case of constant investment opportunity set such that all return distribution parameters are constant. In this case, neither expected returns of assets nor any elements of the covariance matrix move with the state variables. Mathematically, this corresponds to the case when $\nu = 0$.[21] Under these conditions, investors will hold a well-diversified portfolio of risky assets only for the purpose of being compensated by a risk premium.

---

[19] For example, consider the utility function $U(W) = \frac{(W - W_f)^{1-\kappa}}{1-\kappa}$, where $\kappa > 0$, and W_f is a preselected constant. The relative risk aversion, defined as $-\frac{U''W}{U'}$, is equal to $\frac{\kappa}{1 - W_f/W}$, which decreases with wealth such that when the level of wealth is high, relative risk aversion is low, which in turn implies that relative risk tolerance is high. In this case, the investor is willing to take more risk with a higher level of wealth, and less risk with a lower level of wealth, which is what a portfolio insurer will do. W_f can be interpreted as the floor level of wealth at which the investor becomes infinitely risk-averse.

[20] See Merton (1969) and Merton (1990), Chapter 5 for details.

[21] When expected returns and covariance matrix are constant, it can be shown that the prices of risky assets have lognormal distributions. Furthermore, the preference function J will depend only on the level of wealth and time, and no longer on the prices of assets.

Logarithmic Utility Function

The less obvious case is when investor preference can be characterized by a logarithmic utility function, corresponding to the case of $\kappa = 0$ in equation (2.3). It has been shown that the functional form of the optimal portfolio rule in equation (2.5) with a logarithmic utility function is identical to that of a constant investment opportunity set, and is thus also identical to a one-period, myopic mean-variance optimization, except that all expected returns and the covariance matrix are evaluated at the current prices of the risky assets. In any event, there is no intertemporal hedging component in the portfolio rule.

2.3   Tactical Asset Allocation in Practice: One-Period Myopic Analysis

We know of no commercial or practical applications of intertemporal analysis in the investment industry; it is too complex. To appreciate the complexity of applying an intertemporal tactical asset allocation rule, consider a global portfolio of stocks and bonds of the G7 countries. With cash as an additional asset, there are altogether fifteen distinct risky assets in the portfolio.[22] For simplicity, assume that the covariance matrix is constant through time so that state variables affect only expected returns, and all returns are currency-hedged to negate the risk and returns of currencies.

In a study of risk and predictability of international equity returns, Ferson and Harvey (1993) find that returns of the developed stock markets can be predicted by a set of common global variables, such as lagged world equity return, world dividend yield, and interest rate variables, as well as a set of local variables specific to each individual country. Their results are confirmed by subsequent studies. If there are five common global state variables for all countries, and each country has, say, three unique state variables that affect stock returns, there are about twenty-five state variables for expected stock returns in a G-7 portfolio. Similarly, in a study on expected returns of international bond markets, Ilmanen (1995) finds some global and local factors to have information for future bond return dynamics.

All this evidence together suggests that we may need some fifty state variables in order to capture the expected returns of stock and bond markets in a global portfolio with seven countries. It is not difficult to see that the dimension of this realistic asset allocation problem is far beyond what the current computing technology can handle such that the optimal dynamic portfolio strategy in equation (2.5) cannot be solved numerically.

Brennan, Schwartz, and Lagnado (1997, p. 1378) correctly point out that in the investment industry:

---

[22]Note that cash is risk-free only in a one-period model. With multiple periods, the only risk-free asset is the one that has zero covariance with the intertemporal marginal rate of substitution.

Tactical Asset Allocation is essentially a single-period or myopic strategy; it assumes that the decision maker has a (mean-variance) criterion defined over the one-period rate of return on the portfolio.

To bridge the gap between the theoretically optimal intertemporal portfolio rule of equation (2.5) and the more practical but myopic, one-period analysis of tactical asset allocation, one has to assume either that the investment opportunity set is constant, or that investors' preference is well represented by a logarithmic utility function. Neither of these is compelling as there is ample evidence of time-varying expected returns, and a logarithmic utility function is too restrictive.[23]

In addition, strictly speaking, tactical asset allocation is not a very meaningful concept in a one-period world. Asset allocation is "tactical" only when we are comparing asset allocation decisions in different periods, and thus we are using a multi-period setting to think about the issue.

Partly because of its complexity, tactical asset allocation in practice is not quite the same as in theory. The one-period setting is widely used to argue for the importance of tactical asset allocation, as well as for designing trading rule for its implementation.[24]

We therefore analyze tactical asset allocation hereafter in a positive sense, as if it were a myopic strategy, realizing that the resulting rule is optimal only under very particular conditions. More likely, the resulting rule is suboptimal, as it deals with a stochastic investment opportunity set, while, on the other hand, there is no attempt to hedge unfavorable conditions.

Our analysis takes two perspectives. The first one is the total return/total risk perspective, in which investors care about the total return and total risk of the portfolio. The second one is the active return/active risk perspective, in which investors care about the excess return of the portfolio relative to a preselected benchmark and with respect to its variability.

2.3.1   Total Return/Total Risk Perspective

We assume that it is sufficient to express the utility function in terms of the expected return and variance of the portfolio. We call this a *total return/total risk* perspective.

Following von Neumann and Morgenstern (1947), the investor's objective is to maximize the expected utility of wealth. With further standard simplifying assumptions that asset returns follow a multivariate normal distribution and that the investor has constant relative risk aversion, the expected utility of wealth can be characterized by

$$E\left[U\left(W\right)\right] = -\exp\left\{-\gamma\left(E\left[R_p\right] - \frac{\gamma}{2}\sigma_p^2\right)\right\} \qquad (2.17)$$

---

[23] A richer class of utility functions is known as the hyperbolic absolute risk aversion (HARA) family, which includes power utility and logarithmic utility, as well as many others as special cases. Again, see Chapter 5 of Merton (1990) for more details.

[24] For example, see Clarke (1997).

where γ is the constant relative risk aversion (CRRA) coefficient, and $E[R_p]$ and σ_p^2 are the expected return and variance of the portfolio, given by

$$E[R_p] = \omega' E[\mathbf{R}] \tag{2.18}$$

and

$$\sigma_p^2 = \omega' \Omega \omega \tag{2.19}$$

where ω denotes the vector of portfolio weights such that $\omega'\mathbf{1} = 1$, and $\mathbf{1}$ is a vector of ones.

We follow Sharpe (1987) in assuming a constant relative risk aversion. With this assumption, we are able to express the investor's utility in terms of the mean and variance of return, instead of in terms of the investor's wealth. The problem becomes a standard mean-variance analysis. γ can be interpreted as the investor's attitude toward the return-risk trade-off such that the reciprocal of γ is known as the relative risk tolerance.

Maximizing the expected utility given by equation (2.17) is equivalent to solving:

$$\max_{\omega} \omega' E[\mathbf{R}] - \frac{\gamma}{2} \omega' \Omega \omega \tag{2.20}$$

subject to $\omega'\mathbf{1} = 1$

By forming the standard LaGrangian as

$$L = \omega' E[\mathbf{R}] - \frac{\gamma}{2} \omega' \Omega \omega - \lambda(\omega'\mathbf{1} - 1) \tag{2.21}$$

where λ is a LaGrangian multiplier, we can obtain the first-order conditions as

$$\frac{\partial L}{\partial \omega} = E[\mathbf{R}] - \gamma \Omega \omega - \lambda \mathbf{1} = 0 \tag{2.22}$$

$\Longrightarrow$

$$\omega^* = \frac{\Omega^{-1}}{\gamma}(E[\mathbf{R}] - \lambda \mathbf{1}) \tag{2.23}$$

and

$$\frac{\partial L}{\partial \lambda} = -(\omega'\mathbf{1} - 1) = 0 \tag{2.24}$$

$\Longrightarrow$

$$\omega'\mathbf{1} = 1 \tag{2.25}$$

Substituting equation (2.23) into equation (2.25) and rearranging, we obtain

$$\lambda = \frac{\mathbf{1}'\Omega^{-1}E[\mathbf{R}]}{\mathbf{1}'\Omega^{-1}\mathbf{1}} - \frac{\gamma}{\mathbf{1}'\Omega^{-1}\mathbf{1}} \tag{2.26}$$

The vector of optimal portfolio weights can be solved by substituting equation (2.26) into equation (2.23) as

$$\omega^* = \left(1 - \frac{1'\Omega^{-1}E[\mathbf{R}]}{\gamma}\right)\frac{\Omega^{-1}1}{1'\Omega^{-1}1} + \left(\frac{1'\Omega^{-1}E[\mathbf{R}]}{\gamma}\right)\frac{\Omega^{-1}E[\mathbf{R}]}{1'\Omega^{-1}E[\mathbf{R}]} \qquad (2.27)$$

Equation (2.27) is the well-known *Mutual Fund Separation Theorem*, which states that in a mean-variance framework, an optimal portfolio is simply a combination of two distinct portfolios or mutual funds whose portfolio compositions are given by $\frac{\Omega^{-1}1}{1'\Omega^{-1}1}$ and $\frac{\Omega^{-1}E[\mathbf{R}]}{1'\Omega^{-1}E[\mathbf{R}]}$, in this case. The weights of these two portfolios in the optimal portfolio are given by $\left(1 - \frac{1'\Omega^{-1}E[\mathbf{R}]}{\gamma}\right)$ and $\frac{1'\Omega^{-1}E[\mathbf{R}]}{\gamma}$.

The first portfolio, $\frac{\Omega^{-1}1}{1'\Omega^{-1}1}$, is known as the *global minimum-variance portfolio*, which is located at the apex of the standard mean-variance frontier. As its name implies, the global minimum-variance portfolio is the portfolio that has the lowest possible variance in the whole universe of risky assets, and it is unique. For the sake of simplifying notation, we define

$$\omega_g = \frac{\Omega^{-1}1}{1'\Omega^{-1}1} \qquad (2.28)$$

To make our argument for tactical asset allocation more appealing, we first rearrange (2.27) to become

$$\omega^* = \omega_g + \frac{\Omega^{-1}}{\gamma}\left(E[\mathbf{R}] - 1\frac{1'\Omega^{-1}E[\mathbf{R}]}{1'\Omega^{-1}1}\right) \qquad (2.29)$$

Then, we introduce the notion of equilibrium by denoting the vector of equilibrium returns by $\overline{\mathbf{R}}$. Typically, an investor with a long investment horizon will use equilibrium returns in picking an optimal portfolio. Statistically speaking, however, the current state is almost surely not at equilibrium. Therefore, in a realistic case, at least one, and most likely, all elements in the vector of expected returns are different from the vector of equilibrium returns. That is, $E[\mathbf{R}] \neq \overline{\mathbf{R}}$.

To illustrate how important tactical asset allocation is requires more matrix algebra. Rather than relegate the derivation to an appendix, we go through the algebra step by step. In fact, there are some valuable insights embedded in the intermediate steps.

We first add and subtract $\overline{\mathbf{R}}$ in the right-hand side of equation (2.29) to get

$$\omega^* = \omega_g + \frac{\Omega^{-1}}{\gamma}\left(E[\mathbf{R}] - \overline{\mathbf{R}} + \overline{\mathbf{R}} - 1\frac{1'\Omega^{-1}\left(E[\mathbf{R}] - \overline{\mathbf{R}} + \overline{\mathbf{R}}\right)}{1'\Omega^{-1}1}\right) \qquad (2.30)$$

which can be rearranged as

$$\begin{aligned}\omega^* = {}& \omega_g + \frac{\Omega^{-1}}{\gamma}\left(\overline{\mathbf{R}} - 1\frac{1'\Omega^{-1}\overline{\mathbf{R}}}{1'\Omega^{-1}1}\right) \\ & + \frac{\Omega^{-1}}{\gamma}\left(E[\mathbf{R}] - \overline{\mathbf{R}} - 1\frac{1'\Omega^{-1}\left(E[\mathbf{R}] - \overline{\mathbf{R}}\right)}{1'\Omega^{-1}1}\right)\end{aligned} \qquad (2.31)$$

Using the identity of $\mathbf{1}'\mathbf{Z}\mathbf{G} = \mathbf{G}'\mathbf{Z}\mathbf{1}$, where $\mathbf{Z}$ is any $n \times n$ symmetric matrix and $\mathbf{G}$ is a $n \times 1$ vector, we can show that

$$
\boldsymbol{\omega}^* = \boldsymbol{\omega}_g + \frac{1}{\gamma} \frac{\Omega^{-1}}{\mathbf{1}'\Omega^{-1}\mathbf{1}} \left(\overline{\mathbf{R}}\mathbf{1}'\Omega^{-1}\mathbf{1} - \mathbf{1}\overline{\mathbf{R}}'\Omega^{-1}\mathbf{1} \right)
$$
$$
+ \frac{\Omega^{-1}}{\gamma\mathbf{1}'\Omega^{-1}\mathbf{1}} \left(\left(E\left[\mathbf{R}\right] - \overline{\mathbf{R}} \right) \mathbf{1}'\Omega^{-1}\mathbf{1} - \mathbf{1} \left(E\left[\mathbf{R}\right] - \overline{\mathbf{R}} \right)' \Omega^{-1}\mathbf{1} \right) \quad (2.32)
$$

$\Longrightarrow$

$$
\boldsymbol{\omega}^* = \boldsymbol{\omega}_g + \frac{1}{\gamma} \frac{\Omega^{-1}\left(\overline{\mathbf{R}}\mathbf{1}' - \mathbf{1}\overline{\mathbf{R}}' \right)\Omega^{-1}}{\mathbf{1}'\Omega^{-1}\mathbf{1}}\mathbf{1} \quad (2.33)
$$
$$
+ \frac{1}{\gamma} \frac{\Omega^{-1}\left(\left(E\left[\mathbf{R}\right] - \overline{\mathbf{R}} \right)\mathbf{1}' - \mathbf{1}\left(E\left[\mathbf{R}\right] - \overline{\mathbf{R}} \right)' \right)\Omega^{-1}}{\mathbf{1}'\Omega^{-1}\mathbf{1}}\mathbf{1}
$$

Equation (2.33) suggests that there are three components in the optimal portfolio. Unfortunately, the meanings and intuition of these components are largely hidden by the matrix algebra. To uncover their implications, we first rewrite the three components as

$$
\boldsymbol{\omega}^* = \boldsymbol{\omega}_g + \boldsymbol{\omega}_S + \boldsymbol{\omega}_T \quad (2.34)
$$

where

$$
\boldsymbol{\omega}_S = \frac{1}{\gamma} \frac{\Omega^{-1}\left(\overline{\mathbf{R}}\mathbf{1}' - \mathbf{1}\overline{\mathbf{R}}' \right)\Omega^{-1}}{\mathbf{1}'\Omega^{-1}\mathbf{1}}\mathbf{1} \quad (2.35)
$$

and

$$
\boldsymbol{\omega}_T = \frac{1}{\gamma} \frac{\Omega^{-1}\left(\left(E\left[\mathbf{R}\right] - \overline{\mathbf{R}} \right)\mathbf{1}' - \mathbf{1}\left(E\left[\mathbf{R}\right] - \overline{\mathbf{R}} \right)' \right)\Omega^{-1}}{\mathbf{1}'\Omega^{-1}\mathbf{1}}\mathbf{1} \quad (2.36)
$$

The subscripts S and T stand for *strategic* and *tactical*.

Then, let us first take a detailed look of the matrix $\left(\overline{\mathbf{R}}\mathbf{1}' - \mathbf{1}\overline{\mathbf{R}}' \right)$:

$$
\left(\overline{\mathbf{R}}\mathbf{1}' - \mathbf{1}\overline{\mathbf{R}}' \right) = \begin{pmatrix} \overline{R_1} \\ \overline{R_2} \\ \cdot \\ \cdot \\ \overline{R_n} \end{pmatrix} \begin{pmatrix} 1 \\ 1 \\ \cdot \\ \cdot \\ 1 \end{pmatrix}' - \begin{pmatrix} 1 \\ 1 \\ \cdot \\ \cdot \\ 1 \end{pmatrix}' \begin{pmatrix} \overline{R_1} \\ \overline{R_2} \\ \cdot \\ \cdot \\ \overline{R_n} \end{pmatrix} \quad (2.37)
$$
$$
= \begin{pmatrix} 0 & \overline{R_{12}} & \cdot & \cdot & \overline{R_{1n}} \\ \overline{R_{21}} & 0 & \cdot & \cdot & \overline{R_{2n}} \\ \cdot & \cdot & \cdot & \cdot & \cdot \\ \cdot & \cdot & \cdot & \cdot & \cdot \\ \overline{R_{n1}} & \cdot & \cdot & \cdot & 0 \end{pmatrix}
$$

where $\overline{R_{ij}} = \overline{R_i} - \overline{R_j}$. The ij-th element of the matrix $\left(\overline{\mathbf{R}}\mathbf{1}' - \mathbf{1}\overline{\mathbf{R}}'\right)$ is actually the equilibrium excess return of asset i versus asset j. It is also straightforward to show that $\omega_S'\mathbf{1} = 0$.

Similarly, one can show that

$$\left((E\,[\mathbf{R}] - \overline{\mathbf{R}})\,\mathbf{1}' - \mathbf{1}\,(E\,[\mathbf{R}] - \overline{\mathbf{R}})'\right) \tag{2.38}$$

$$= \begin{pmatrix} 0 & \cdot & \cdot & E\,[R_{1n}] - \overline{R_{1n}} \\ E\,[R_{21}] - \overline{R_{21}} & \cdot & \cdot & E\,[R_{2n}] - \overline{R_{2n}} \\ \cdot & & \cdot & \cdot \\ \cdot & & \cdot & \cdot \\ E\,[R_{n1}] - \overline{R_{n1}} & \cdot & \cdot & 0 \end{pmatrix}$$

where $E\,[R_{ij}] = E\,[R_i] - E\,[R_j]$.

That is, the ij-th element of $\left((E\,[\mathbf{R}] - \overline{\mathbf{R}})\,\mathbf{1}' - \mathbf{1}\,(E\,[\mathbf{R}] - \overline{\mathbf{R}})'\right)$ is the deviation of expected excess return of asset i versus asset j from equilibrium excess return, and it can be shown that $\omega_A'\mathbf{1} = 0$. With these clarifications, we are better able to interpret equation (2.34).

To maximize expected utility, in addition to just holding the global minimum variance portfolio, the investor needs to make two bets at the beginning of the period: one strategic, one tactical.[25]

Strategic Bet

The first bet is a strategic bet denoted by ω_S. If all assets have exactly the same equilibrium returns, the strategic bet is irrelevant, so the optimal portfolio is simply the global minimum-variance portfolio and a possible tactical bet (to be discussed). If equilibrium returns are different, the investor should then shift some of the holdings of those assets with lower equilibrium returns to assets with higher equilibrium returns. How big the bet is depends on the degree of relative risk tolerance and the covariance matrix, as well as the equilibrium excess returns.

In practice, the combination of ω_g and ω_S is commonly known as the *strategic mix*, or the *policy portfolio*, for the reason that the investor is willing to hold this portfolio for the long run when equilibrium is expected to be attained in steady-state. In the tactical asset allocation industry, this strategic mix is commonly known as the *benchmark portfolio*.

Tactical Bet

The second bet is a tactical bet denoted by ω_T. Expected returns can be different from equilibrium returns. Therefore, when the investor perceives that the current state is not at equilibrium, tactical bets should be made as well in

---

[25] I thank André Perold for observing that, although the derivation is different, my results are largely consistent with Treynor and Black (1973), who use the CAPM as the equilibrium reference point.

order to maximize expected utility. Failing to do so will incur a welfare loss that is measured in expected utility. The size and direction of the bets depend on the degree of relative risk tolerance, the covariance matrix, and the deviations of expected excess returns from equilibrium excess returns. Equation (2.36) is used throughout as the standard representation of a linear tactical trading rule.[26]

Strategic asset allocation decisions are made based on long-term or equilibrium forecasts of returns and risk. The resulting benchmark portfolio is consistent with this set of long-term views on the investment opportunity set as well as the investor's investment and consumption profile. When near term and intermediate-term returns and risk deviate from their equilibrium, the strategic benchmark becomes suboptimal.

As long as we agree that the current state is not at equilibrium, tactical asset allocation is thus relevant. In short, when implemented appropriately, tactical asset allocation steers the investor in the right direction toward optimality.

Pairwise Bet Structure

Equations (2.36) and (2.38) offer some additional important insights on bet structure, which are embedded in the matrix of the equation. Look first at the rows and columns of the matrix $\left[\left(E\left[\mathbf{R} \right] - \overline{\mathbf{R}} \right) \mathbf{1}' - \mathbf{1} \left(E\left[\mathbf{R} \right] - \overline{\mathbf{R}} \right)' \right]$. The j-th element of the i-th row is equal to $\left(E\left[R_i \right] - E\left[R_j \right] \right) - \left(\overline{R_i} - \overline{R_j} \right)$, so that we are comparing asset i to the other $n-1$ assets in each element of the row vector. Similarly, the i-th element of the j-th column is equal to $\left(E\left[R_j \right] - E\left[R_i \right] \right) - \left(\overline{R_j} - \overline{R_i} \right)$, so that we are comparing asset j to the other $n-1$ assets in each element of the column vector. The implicit pairwise bet structure should be obvious; each asset is being compared to another asset in each element of the matrix.

Since no bet is made against the same asset, the pairwise matrix has zeros along its diagonal. The lower triangle and the upper triangle of the matrix are mirror images of each other, as the bet of asset i against asset j is just the opposite of the bet of asset j against asset i. Therefore, the total number of pairwise bets with n assets is equal to the number of elements in the lower or upper triangle of an $n \times n$ matrix, which is $\frac{n(n-1)}{2}$.

To compute the total tactical bets of all assets, the matrix in equation (2.38) has to be first weighted by the inverse of the covariance matrix, Ω^{-1}, through a quadratic form, $\Omega^{-1} \left[\left(E\left[\mathbf{R} \right] - \overline{\mathbf{R}} \right) \mathbf{1}' - \mathbf{1} \left(E\left[\mathbf{R} \right] - \overline{\mathbf{R}} \right)' \right] \Omega^{-1}$. While the relationship between the elements in Ω^{-1} and the elements in the corresponding positions in Ω is more than just a reciprocal, it is generally true that there is an inverse relationship between the two. Therefore, we may interpret the quadratic form as a risk adjustment in accordance with the variances of both assets involved in each pairwise bet as well as their covariance. For the same

---

[26]This tactical trading rule is consistent with the linear investment rules implied by the ergodic hypothesis of Granito (1986).

signal, the bets between pairs of less volatile assets are larger than bets between pairs of more volatile assets. To further adjust the aggressiveness of the tactical portfolio, the whole structure is multiplied by the relative risk tolerance, $\frac{1}{\gamma}$, and then by the scalar $\frac{1}{1'\Omega^{-1}1}$. Finally, the risk-adjusted pairwise comparisons of deviations of expected returns from equilibrium are summed together through matrix multiplication with the unit vector, $\mathbf{1}$.

Example: A World of Two Risky Assets

We can illustrate our argument using a two-asset example. With only two assets in the investment universe, we largely bypass the complicated matrix algebra.

Assume that there are only two risky assets in the investment universe, say, stocks and bonds. According to equation (2.33), the optimal portfolio weights in asset 1 and asset 2 are:

$$
\begin{aligned}
\omega_1^* \;=\; & \frac{\sigma_2^2 - \rho\sigma_1\sigma_2}{\sigma_1^2 + \sigma_2^2 - 2\rho\sigma_1\sigma_2} + \frac{1}{\gamma}\frac{\overline{R_1} - \overline{R_2}}{\sigma_1^2 + \sigma_2^2 - 2\rho\sigma_1\sigma_2} \\
& + \frac{1}{\gamma}\frac{\left(E\left[R_1\right] - E\left[R_2\right]\right) - \left(\overline{R_1} - \overline{R_2}\right)}{\sigma_1^2 + \sigma_2^2 - 2\rho\sigma_1\sigma_2}
\end{aligned}
\tag{2.39}
$$

and

$$
\begin{aligned}
\omega_2^* \;=\; & 1 - \omega_1^* \\
\;=\; & \frac{\sigma_1^2 - \rho\sigma_1\sigma_2}{\sigma_1^2 + \sigma_2^2 - 2\rho\sigma_1\sigma_2} + \frac{1}{\gamma}\frac{\overline{R_2} - \overline{R_1}}{\sigma_1^2 + \sigma_2^2 - 2\rho\sigma_1\sigma_2} \\
& + \frac{1}{\gamma}\frac{\left(E\left[R_2\right] - E\left[R_1\right]\right) - \left(\overline{R_2} - \overline{R_1}\right)}{\sigma_1^2 + \sigma_2^2 - 2\rho\sigma_1\sigma_2}
\end{aligned}
\tag{2.40}
$$

The first terms are the weights of asset 1 and asset 2 in the global minimum-variance portfolio. It is intuitive that the less volatile asset has a higher weight, as it is required to maintain a lower variance of the portfolio. If asset 1 has a higher variance than asset 2, $\sigma_1^2 > \sigma_2^2$, the first terms in the above equations suggest that the global minimum-variance portfolio will give more weight to asset 2, and vice versa.

The second terms are the strategic bets on the equilibrium excess return of asset 1 over asset 2, and vice versa. If asset 1 has a higher equilibrium return, it should be overweighted with respect to the global minimum-variance portfolio, so asset 2 should be underweighted.

Finally, the third terms are the tactical bets on the current deviation of expected excess return from its equilibrium.

We thus have some interesting insights into how a neutral stance in tactical asset allocation should be defined. The optimal rule of tactical asset allocation, according to equation (2.36), appears to be to trade the deviation of pairwise expected excess return from equilibrium. The resulting portfolio strategy is ex-ante mean-variance efficient.

Therefore, a tactical asset allocation manager should not overweight stock simply because the equilibrium return of stocks is higher than the equilibrium return of bonds, for this piece of information is already incorporated in the strategic bet. Although this structural bet is very likely to add value over a reasonable period of time such that stocks outperform bonds during the period, this result has nothing to do with the information set of the manager.

2.3.2 Active Return/Active Risk Perspective

We have assumed that the investor measures utility by the total return and total risk of the portfolio as in equation (2.17) so that we can specify the objective function in terms of expected return and variance of the portfolio. This specification may make sense from the perspective of an investor who cares about the level of wealth, which is determined by the performance of the overall portfolio, including the strategic benchmark portfolio decisions and the tactical asset allocation decisions.

The investment industry, however, typically evaluates and rewards managers on the basis of their performance versus their benchmark portfolios. That is, performance is measured according to the level and variability of excess return relative to a benchmark. In order to remain competitive, managers compensated this way are more likely to focus on active return and active risk, rather than on the total return and total risk of the portfolio.

Managers typically educate their clients about the importance of a portfolio's mean-variance efficiency. In doing so, they have probably presented to their clients the positions of numerous different combinations of assets in the mean-variance space. It is hard to imagine, though, that a manager can be successful in gaining new business or retaining existing business only by improving mean-variance efficiency at the expense of lower total return. A manager who fails to deliver positive excess return relative to the benchmark portfolio is not likely to remain competitive.

We can revisit the one-period mean-variance analysis of tactical asset allocation by taking a different perspective. Instead of focusing on the total return and total risk of the overall portfolio, let us assume that only the active return and active risk of the tactical positions count. That is, it is sufficient to express the expected utility function in terms of alpha, defined as the excess return relative to the benchmark, and tracking error, defined as the standard deviation of alpha. Similar type of analysis for active portfolio management is analyzed by Roll (1992), who puts more focus on the implications of portfolio's mean-variance efficiency.[27]

We are more interested in the bet structure instead. Let **Bet** be the $n \times 1$ vector of tactical bets on each asset i in the portfolio, with elements Bet_i, $i = 1, 2, ..., n$. That is, Bet_i measures the deviation of asset i's portfolio weight from the benchmark. Maintaining the assumption of either a quadratic utility

---

[27]Note that Roll (1992) uses the terms "tracking error" and "standard deviation of tracking error" for what most practitioners in the investment industry typically call "alpha" and "tracking error."

function, or that alphas from different tactical bets follow a multivariate normal distribution, and a constant relative risk aversion for tracking error, the expected utility can be characterized by

$$E\left[U\right] = -\exp\left\{-\gamma_T\left(\alpha - \frac{\gamma_T}{2}TE^2\right)\right\} \tag{2.41}$$

where γ_T is the constant relative risk aversion coefficient for tracking error, and α and TE^2 are the alpha and variance of the alpha from the tactical strategy, given by

$$\alpha = \mathbf{Bet}'E\left[\mathbf{R}\right] \tag{2.42}$$

and

$$\begin{aligned} TE^2 &= Var\left(\alpha\right) \\ &= \mathbf{Bet}'\Omega\mathbf{Bet} \end{aligned} \tag{2.43}$$

γ_T is known as the relative risk tolerance for tracking error, which measures the trade-off between alpha and tracking error, TE. The subscript T stands for *tactical*, in order to distinguish it from the case with total return and total risk.[28] Since attitudes toward total risk measured by γ in equation (2.17) can differ from attitudes toward active risk of tracking error, it is entirely possible that $\gamma \neq \gamma_T$.

Again, the portfolio problem can be solved with standard mean-variance analysis, but with alpha and tracking error instead of return and variance of the portfolio. The problem can be stated as

$$\max_{\mathbf{Bet}} \mathbf{Bet}'E\left[\mathbf{R}\right] - \frac{\gamma_T}{2}\mathbf{Bet}'\Omega\mathbf{Bet} \tag{2.44}$$

subject to $\mathbf{Bet}'\mathbf{1} = 0$

where $\mathbf{1}$ is a vector of ones. Other than putting alpha and tracking error in the objective function, the noticeable difference is the fact that the sum of all tactical bets, denoted by $\sum_{i=1}^{n} Bet_i = \mathbf{Bet}'\mathbf{1}$, is zero.

We form the standard LaGrangian as

$$L = \mathbf{Bet}'E\left[\mathbf{R}\right] - \frac{\gamma_T}{2}\mathbf{Bet}'\Omega\mathbf{Bet} - \lambda_T\mathbf{Bet}'\mathbf{1} \tag{2.45}$$

where λ_T is a LaGrangian multiplier. Taking derivatives and solving the resulting first-order conditions gives the optimal solution for the tactical bets vector as

$$\mathbf{Bet}^* = \frac{1}{\gamma_T}\frac{\Omega^{-1}\left(E\left[\mathbf{R}\right]\mathbf{1}' - \mathbf{1}E\left[\mathbf{R}\right]'\right)\Omega^{-1}}{\mathbf{1}'\Omega^{-1}\mathbf{1}}\mathbf{1} \tag{2.46}$$

---

[28]The subscript T used for tactical here should not be confused with the same subscript used elsewhere to denote the number of time periods.

If the benchmark portfolio is represented as $\omega_g + \omega_S$ as implied in equation (2.34), the total portfolio position can be denoted as $\omega_g + \omega_S + \mathbf{Bet}^*$.

An inspection of equation (2.46) for $\mathbf{Bet}^*$ and equation (2.36) for ω^* should reveal that the two solutions have very similar forms, and the pairwise bet structure is retained. Other than the fact that now it is the relative risk tolerance for active risk, $\frac{1}{\gamma_T}$, that matters, the most important difference is the absence of the vector of equilibrium returns, $\overline{\mathbf{R}}$, in the optimal tactical bet when alpha and tracking error are of concern.

Recall that the benchmark portfolio compositions are determined by the equilibrium returns, covariance matrix, and the investor's attitude toward risk. This implies that, *when only alpha and tracking error matter in the objective function, the optimal tactical bets are completely independent of the benchmark portfolio*. Or, in contrast to equation (2.36), where mean-variance efficiency of the overall portfolio is maximized such that the optimal tactical bets are determined by the deviations of excess returns from their equilibrium values, the tactical bets under optimization of alpha and tracking error are independent of the equilibrium returns. The optimal tactical bets are instead determined solely by the current expected returns of the assets and the covariance matrix.

In other words, provided that the other parameters are the same, a manager should make exactly the same trades from an initial position in the benchmark for all clients, even though their benchmark portfolios can be very different.

By definition, the resulting portfolio will be mean-variance efficient if and only if the optimal portfolio compositions are solved according to mean-variance optimization of total return and total risk. Consequently, the overall portfolio, $\omega_g + \omega_S + \omega_T$, under the total return/total risk perspective will be mean-variance efficient, while the portfolio, $\omega_g + \omega_S + \mathbf{Bet}^*$, under the active return/active risk perspective will be mean-variance inefficient, a result consistent with Roll (1992).

2.4 Concluding Remarks: Equilibrium and Strategic Benchmark

A client hires an asset allocation manager. With the help of the manager, the client chooses a mix of 60% stock and 40% cash as the strategic benchmark portfolio. TAA is then implemented as an overlay based on the manager's proprietary information and skills. Thirty years later, the manager gives a performance review. Performance is great, and the manager adds significant value. The client notices that the average portfolio position in stock is 90%, while the average position in cash is 10%.

"Why is the average position in stock so much higher than my benchmark? With a thirty-year horizon, aren't you supposed to have added value just by putting more of my money in stock? That's what I read in Siegel's (1998) book," the client says.

"Well, we have superior asset allocation skills, and we have a lot of information on stock returns. According to finance theory, everything else equal, investors who have better information on stock should hold more stock than the others. See Barberis (1999), Brandt (1999), and Campbell and Viceira (1999), for example," the manager answers.[29]

"Why didn't you tell me thirty years ago? I would have picked my benchmark as 90%/10%, and you should have done TAA from that," is the the client's response.

This example illustrates some practical issues in picking a strategic benchmark portfolio. Putting aside client specific considerations, returns and the covariance matrix are the critical inputs for the determination of an appropriate benchmark in current investment management. Ask five prospective managers to submit their portfolio frontiers, and you will see that no two frontiers are the same. Why?

The managers must have used different returns or covariance matrices, or both. Some may have used the historical average of the last ten or twenty years, while others may have used some subjective projections of the future. The point is, all portfolio frontiers are subjective; they are conditional on the manager's information set. In other words, to some degree, the manager's information is implicitly incorporated into the benchmark portfolio.

So, how much and what kind of manager information should be incorporated when choosing the benchmark? Should, in the above example, the manager and the client have jointly picked 90%/10% as the benchmark, instead of the 60%/40%? While there is really no good rule of thumb, the potential implications of a structural bet should not be overlooked.[30]

For instance, the client hires manager A for implementing TAA on a 60%/40% benchmark. Manager A happens to have absolutely no information advantage to add value through TAA. To add value, manager A first overweights stock by 10% all the time. On top of that, a random bet is made based on a noise drawn from a unit-normal distribution with zero mean. Then, manager A outsources a benchmark portfolio of 70%/30% to manager B for running TAA. Coincidentally, manager B is also ignorant of TAA. To retain the business, manager B makes a structural bet by constantly overweighting stock by 5% plus a random bet based on a unit-normal, and also outsources a benchmark portfolio of 75%/25% to manager C for running TAA. If this goes on and on, it is not difficult to see that, at the end, the client's average position in stock will be close to 100%, but yet, after a long enough horizon, all the managers outperform the benchmark assigned to them with no information advantage!

Unfortunately, it is virtually impossible to distinguish whether a structural

---

[29] Another way to understand this issue is to think about the risk of stock. If the manager has perfect information on stock returns, one can argue that stock is riskless, even though its return is volatile. In this case, while the unconditional variance of stock is simply its historical variance, the conditional variance, computed as the variance of the unexpected component of stock return, will be lower. Therefore, the conditional portfolio frontier of an investor with good information is shifted to the left. Everything else equal, the conditional risk of stock is lower, and thus the portfolio holdings of stock will be higher.

[30] We define stuctural bet as a nonzero average bet on any one asset class. The structural bet in the example is +30% on stock, and -30% on cash.

bet is an intentional uninformed bet, or the result of some changing investment opportunity set such as a secular decline of risk or the "new paradigm" argument.[31]

Dictionary definitions of equilibrium include:

"A condition in which all acting influences are canceled by others, resulting in a stable, balanced, or unchanging system."

"Emotional or mental balance."

Hereafter, we interpret equilibrium distribution assumptions as the set of assumptions of returns and the covariance matrix with which the client and asset allocation manager jointly determine the appropriate strategic benchmark portfolio after incorporating the available information set. Given this benchmark portfolio, the manager should have no reason to make a structural bet, and tactical bets are made only when the investment opportunity set deviates from the equilibrium. While this definition may be case-specific, it greatly simplifies the discussion of structural bets in Chapters 4, 5, and 6.

My first economics professor, Professor Andrew G. Verzilli, believed that economics can be, and should be, taught to kindergarten children. In one class, after he explained the X curve of supply and demand, he asked the students what they saw as "equilibrium." A five-year-old girl raised her hand, and answered, "It is the point of happiness."

---

[31] It is not difficult to notice that some strategists rarely recommend underweighting stocks in their portfolios for two decades. One tactical asset allocation manager's book shows that stock has been overweighted against cash about 90% of the time in the last twenty-five years. There is no way, however, to accuse managers of making an uninformed structural bet on stock, as the average overweight could be the results of other factors. Nevertheless, their performance are extraordinarily impressive, though.

Chapter 3

Performance Measures

3.1 Introduction

This chapter discusses some commonly used measures in the investment industry for evaluation of asset allocation managers, including alpha, tracking error, the information ratio, and the hit ratio. We also discuss the strengths and weaknesses of the Henriksson-Merton measure and the Cumby-Modest measure for market timing; they are sometimes used as alternative evaluation measures. Finally, we use two proprietary signals for stock-bond pairwise decisions to illustrate implementation of these performance measures.

3.2 Alpha

In the investment industry, the excess return due to active decisions is generally known as alpha. Its likely origin is the term "Jensen's alpha" in the finance literature, where alpha denotes the intercept term in a regression for evaluation of performance.[1] While Jensen's alpha is related to beta adjustment, the customary definition of alpha in the industry has nothing to do with beta. Investment alpha depends instead on the benchmark and the actively managed portfolio.

Although the definition may be simple, computing alpha is not as straightforward. The problems largely arise from our assumptions as to how the excess return in each period is reinvested, as well as the choice for annualization.[2]

Suppose there are two portfolios, which invest in only two assets, stocks and bonds, for example. Each portfolio starts with the same principal initial investments, W. The first portfolio has fixed compositions of stocks and bonds, and at the end of each period, it is rebalanced to the constant weights, denoted as ω and $(1 - \omega)$, respectively. This portfolio is known as the benchmark portfolio. The second portfolio, called TAA, is the tactical asset allocation portfolio, where

---

[1] See Jensen (1969).

[2] A relevant discussion on the subject is Goodwin (1998). We also investigate the effects of aggressiveness factors and the underlying assumptions on annualizing tracking error.

the portfolio composition is changed at the end of each period in accordance with the signals and portfolio construction procedures. As there is only one pairwise bet in the portfolio, Portfolio TAA's compositions can be denoted as $(\omega + Bet_t)$ and $(1 - \omega - Bet_t)$ in stocks and bonds, respectively. The bet at each period depends on the signals, as well as the aggressiveness of the strategy. We measure the aggressiveness by the *aggressiveness factor*, which can simply be viewed as a multiple of the signal in order to scale the signal into a bet. For example, if the signal is 1%, then the bet will be 1% if the aggressiveness factor is 1. Similarly, the bet will be 10% if the aggressiveness factor is 10.

The return of the benchmark portfolio in each period is

$$R_t = \omega R_{S,t} + (1 - \omega) R_{B,t} \tag{3.1}$$

The return of the tactical portfolio in period t depends on the tactical bet made in the previous period, $t - 1$, and is given by

$$R_{TAA,t} = (\omega + Bet_{t-1}) R_{S,t} + (1 - \omega - Bet_{t-1}) R_{B,t} \tag{3.2}$$

By definition, alpha is the excess return due to the active asset allocation bet, which is calculated as

$$\begin{aligned} \alpha_t &= R_{TAA,t} - R_t \tag{3.3} \\ &= Bet_{t-1} (R_{S,t} - R_{B,t}) \tag{3.4} \end{aligned}$$

Although the time series of alpha during the whole sample period can be informative, it is rarely used for evaluating managers. Instead, a single number such as an average alpha within the period is used for comparison of managers. Typically, an annualized alpha is reported by each manager. There are many different ways to annualize, each with particular strengths and drawbacks. Compliance with the Association for Investment Management and Research (AIMR) performance presentation standards requires that all investment results be reported in terms of geometric rather than arithmetic average returns. As a result, geometric returns have more or less become the standard for the investment industry.

We briefly discuss three common techniques for annualization. Hereafter, α without a time subscript denotes the average alpha of the sample period with T periods.

While the alpha in each period shows the excess return from the strategy, it is typically too volatile to be useful for revealing the skill of the manager. The standard practice in the industry is to smooth the alphas over a certain horizon. Annualized alpha is by far the most commonly used measure, although longer-horizon measures such as three-year alpha are also used.

It is important to distinguish "annualized" and "annual" performance measures. The former describes the practice when we do not have enough actual annual observations to compute the latter. To annualize monthly alphas, for example, the manager computes the annualized alpha in each rolling twelve-month period based on the monthly alphas in the previous twelve months. In reality, no managers have enough years of live performance to compute annual performance measures. Since the annualized measure largely mitigates the inter-month volatility of alphas, it is more smooth, and thus may be a better measure for the true skill of the manager.

3.2.1 Geometric Mean

Geometric alpha incorporates the effects of compounding in each period. It is indeed a better measure of the actual return on investment and the standard measure of the AIMR. There are two commonly used methodologies to calculate geometric alpha.

Method 1

The first method requires calculation of geometric average returns of the benchmark portfolio and the active portfolio separately during the same period of time. The annualized geometric average returns of the two portfolios are calculated as

$$R_G = 12 \left[\prod_{t=1}^{T} (1 + R_t) \right]^{\frac{1}{T}} - 1 \tag{3.5}$$

and

$$R_{TAA,G} = 12 \left[\prod_{t=1}^{T} (1 + R_{TAA,t}) \right]^{\frac{1}{T}} - 1 \tag{3.6}$$

where the subscript G denotes geometric, and $\prod$ is the multiplication operator. The geometric alpha is then computed as the difference of the geometric average returns:

$$\alpha_G = R_{TAA,G} - R_G \tag{3.7}$$

In calculating the geometric mean, the return of the benchmark portfolio in each period is compounded, making it a better indication of the accumulation of wealth. This strength, however, also gives rise to its many drawbacks.

First, it is benchmark-dependent. As a result, the same set of information and signals, when applied to make tactical bets with different benchmark portfolios, can lead to very different annualized alphas. This makes fair comparison of the performance of different managers or strategies more difficult without an explicit statement of the benchmark portfolios in each strategy. Managers typically have some representative benchmark portfolios, which can be quite different from each other. Some typical examples include 60/30/10, 65/30/5, or 60/40/0 in stocks/bonds/cash. Even though two managers report the same annualized alpha of 2%, their numbers can have different meanings. In addition, one cannot determine what the manager's alpha would have been if the benchmark had been 60/40/0 instead of 60/30/10.

Second, unlike the arithmetic mean, the geometric mean is not a simple linear function of the degree of aggressiveness, meaning that the annualized alpha of a strategy with twice the degree of aggressiveness is not exactly double. Whether it is more than or less than double is unpredictable, as all return shocks in each period of time count. A large return shock can either help or hurt the more aggressive strategy, which causes its annualized alpha to be higher or lower.

Finally, it is considerably more complicated to calculate.

Method 2

The second method is probably the less popular method.[3] The geometric alpha is defined as

$$\alpha_G = \left[\prod_{t=1}^{T} \left(\frac{1 + R_{TAA,t}}{1 + R_t} \right) \right]^{\frac{12}{T}} - 1 \tag{3.8}$$

As returns in each period are compounded, it has properties similar to the first method, and the similar drawbacks for comparing managers' performance.

3.2.2 Arithmetic Mean

The easiest way to calculate annualized alpha, although not necessarily the most common, is to use the arithmetic mean. For example, assume that tactical bets are made at the end of each month from $t = 1$ to $t = T$. The annualized alpha is calculated as

$$\alpha_A = \frac{12}{T} \sum_{t=1}^{T} \alpha_t \tag{3.9}$$

where the subscript A denotes arithmetic. Here, according to equation (3.3), annualized alpha based on arithmetic mean is independent of the benchmark portfolio's compositions. In addition, annualized alpha becomes a simple multiple of the aggressiveness factor. This can easily be verified from equation (3.4). As the strategy becomes twice as aggressive (doubling the aggressiveness factor), so is the bet at each time period. Therefore, the annualized alpha will also be double.

Besides being the simplest to calculate, these features related to independence of benchmark portfolio and the aggressiveness factor make the arithmetic alpha a much better measure for analysis. One may interpret the arithmetic mean measure as the profitability measure of a zero net cost, long-short, arbitrage portfolio with no reinvestment of alpha. Unlike the geometric mean measure, in which alpha in each period is reinvested and compounded in the current portfolio, which is the benchmark portfolio plus all the bets, the arithmetic mean measure implies that all positions in each period have to be liquidated.

---

[3] See Goodwin (1998).

Because we are most concerned with comparison of different signals and managers, we use the arithmetic alpha for annualization of alpha unless otherwise stated. We acknowledge that to measure actual investment return and wealth accumulation, the geometric alpha is better.

3.3 Tracking Error

Even if a strategy delivers positive alpha on average over a sample period, it is important to know how consistent its performance is in each period of time. In other words, we also need to understand the *dispersion* of alphas. In statistics, degree of dispersion is typically measured by the standard deviation. By definition, the tracking error of a strategy is the standard deviation of alphas. That is:

$$TE_t = \sqrt{\frac{1}{T-1} \sum_{t=1}^{T} \left(\alpha_t - \frac{1}{T} \sum_{t=1}^{T} \alpha_t \right)^2} \qquad (3.10)$$

The subscript t is used to distinguish tracking error from the annualized tracking error discussed below. Note that TE_t is not a time series, but rather a single time-average measure for the time series of α_t.

3.3.1 Annualized Tracking Error

Similar to the reporting of annualized alpha, tracking error is usually reported in an annualized form. Although it is not formally the industry standard, practically almost all managers annualize their tracking error by multiplying it by the square root of the number of analysis time periods in a year. That is:

$$TE = \sqrt{\text{number of periods in a year}} \times TE_t \qquad (3.11)$$

TE without a subscript denotes the annualized tracking error. For example, if bets are made monthly so that the tracking error is the standard deviation of monthly alphas, annualized tracking error is equal to $\sqrt{12} \times$ monthly tracking error. Similarly, if bets are made weekly, annualized tracking error is equal to $\sqrt{52} \times$ weekly tracking error.

3.3.2 Implicit Assumption: Time-Independence of Alpha

In the investment industry, annualization of tracking error has become so mechanical that the important implicit assumption made is rarely emphasized. To articulate the issue, we need to review time-series analysis. While the point can easily be made with continuous-time mathematics, we use discrete-time analysis to make it accessible to a wider range of readers.

Annualized tracking error according to equation (3.11) is the product of the tracking error and the square root of the number of periods in a year. In other words, the standard deviation of alpha grows with the square root of time, or the variance of alpha grows linearly with time. The analysis below shows that this is true if and only if alphas are serially independent. That is, alphas in different periods of time are independent.

We begin with a simple two-period example: the variance of a two-period return. For simplicity, we analyze continuously compounded return such that a two-period return is equal to the sum of two consecutive one-period returns. That is,

$$R_{t-2,t} = R_{t-2,t-1} + R_{t-1,t} \qquad (3.12)$$

The variance of this two-period return can be computed as

$$
\begin{aligned}
Var\left(R_{t-2,t}\right) &= Var\left(R_{t-2,t-1} + R_{t-1,t}\right) \\
&= Var\left(R_{t-2,t-1}\right) + Var\left(R_{t-1,t}\right) \\
&\quad +2Cov\left(R_{t-2,t-1}, R_{t-1,t}\right) \\
&= 2Var\left(R_{t-1,t}\right) + 2Cov\left(R_{t-2,t-1}, R_{t-1,t}\right) \qquad (3.13)
\end{aligned}
$$

That is, the variance of the two-period return is equal to twice the variance of the one-period return plus twice the covariance between two consecutive one-period returns. To generalize the argument for longer periods, it is easier to compare the ratio of a q-period return to q times the variance of a one-period return. In the case of two-period return, we write that

$$VR\left(2\right) = \frac{Var\left(R_{t-2,t}\right)}{2Var\left(R_{t-1,t}\right)} = 1 + 2\rho\left(1\right) \qquad (3.14)$$

where $VR\left(2\right)$ denotes a two-period variance ratio, and $\rho\left(1\right)$ is the first-order autocorrelation coefficient of one-period returns.

When returns are positively autocorrelated, meaning that a higher-than-average return tends to be followed by another higher-than-average return while a lower-than-average return tends to be followed by another lower-than-average return, $VR\left(2\right)$ is greater than one, implying that the variance of a two-period return exceeds twice the variance of a one-period return. In other words, variance grows faster than linearly with time. When returns are negatively autocorrelated, the opposite is true, meaning that variance grows less than linearly with time.

With a similar calculation, it can be shown that the q-period variance ratio is given by

$$VR\left(q\right) = \frac{Var\left(R_{t-q,t}\right)}{qVar\left(R_{t-1,t}\right)} = 1 + 2\sum_{i=1}^{q-1}\left(1 - \frac{i}{q}\right)\rho\left(i\right) \qquad (3.15)$$

To illustrate the implication of equation (3.15), consider the case of annualizing monthly tracking error into annual tracking error, that is, for $q = 12$.

$$Var(\alpha_{t-12,t}) = \left(1 + 2 \times \frac{11}{12}\rho(1) + 2 \times \frac{10}{12}\rho(2) + ... + 2 \times \frac{1}{12}\rho(11)\right)$$
$$\times 12 Var(\alpha_{t-1,t}) \tag{3.16}$$

Therefore, the variance of annual alpha is equal to 12 times the variance of monthly alpha if and only if the value in the parentheses is exactly equal to one, or, when the weighted sum of higher-order autocorrelation coefficients of monthly alpha up to the 11-th order is exactly zero. In any event, it is obvious that annualization of tracking error by the square root of number of periods in a year misestimates risk, or the dispersion of annual alpha.

To shed light on whether annual tracking error is more likely to be overstated or understated, we have to look into the details of how one-period alpha is calculated. Generally, alpha in a particular time period is equal to the product of the bet at the end of the previous period and the difference in returns of the pair of assets in this period, such as in equation (3.4). As a result, autocorrelation of alpha will likely come from autocorrelation of bets or returns, or both. Considerable research indicates that short-horizon returns, such as monthly, are close to serially independent, although there is some mixed evidence on the negative autocorrelations of long-horizon returns, such as three to five years. We can safely assume that returns do not contribute significantly to any serial dependence of alphas.[4]

Bets, on the other hand, are almost certainly positively autocorrelated. For a bet to be serially independent, it has to change signs so frequently that it behaves like a noise series, and it will lead to unacceptable turnover for the portfolio. In addition, since information flow is continuous, managers will tend to change their views on assets, and subsequently their bets, continually and gradually. As a result, tactical bets will have strong positive autocorrelations. In fact, this is consistent with the actual tactical bets reported by all asset allocation managers in the industry.

Putting these pieces together, we can conclude that alphas have positive serial dependence. As a result, annualizing alpha by a multiple of the square root of the number of periods in a year *underestimates* the dispersion of alphas, and therefore underestimates the risk of the tactical strategy measured on an annual basis.

3.4 Information Ratio

We have noted that alphas and tracking errors depend on the aggressiveness factor as well as the skill of the manager. This feature makes comparison of different managers difficult. The fact that the alpha of one manager is higher

---

[4] An easy way to think about why autocorrelations in bets will lead to autocorrelations in alphas even when realized returns are serially independent is in terms of equation (3.4). If the realized risk premium between stock and bond is a constant plus a random noise, any serial dependence in bets, to some extent, will be preserved in serial dependence in alphas.

than others does not necessarily suggest that this manager has the best skill, as the manager may simply be the most aggressiven in making bets. As the degree of aggressiveness increases, alphas will also be more disperse, leading to a higher tracking error as well as higher alpha. For a fair comparison of different managers, we need some measures that are more or less aggressiveness-independent. One such measure is the information ratio.

The information ratio is defined as the ratio of alpha to tracking error:

$$Information\ Ratio = \frac{Alpha}{Tracking\ Error} \qquad (3.17)$$

Computation of the information ratio depends on which measure of alpha is used, geometric or arithmetic. While geometric mean is a better measure of true performance, we again use the arithmetic mean , largely for its analytical tractability. In later chapters, it should become clear that analytic tractability is critically important in order to derive expressions that are both illuminating and intuitive. Unless it is otherwise stated, all information ratios hereforth are computed on the basis of the arithmetic mean in this book.

As in the case of other performance measures, managers typically report annualized information ratios. To annualize an information ratio from shorter-horizon statistics, we combine equations (3.9), (3.11), and (4.22), which suggests that

$$Annualized\ Information\ Ratio = \frac{Annualized\ Alpha}{Annualized\ Tracking\ Error} \qquad (3.18)$$

For example, to report an annualized information ratio based on monthly alphas and tracking error:

$$Annualized\ Information\ Ratio = \frac{Average\ Monthly\ Alpha}{Monthly\ Tracking\ Error} \times \sqrt{12} \quad (3.19)$$

While the mechanics of computing the information ratio are straightforward, it is well to keep in mind the implicit assumption of the time-independence of alphas and the potential distortion of performance measurement. Since annualized tracking error underestimates the true degree of dispersion of annual alpha, one would expect the annualized information ratio computed this way to overstate the true annual information ratio.

3.5   Hit Ratio

Another aggressiveness- and benchmark-independent performance measure is the hit ratio. The hit ratio is defined as the proportion of times that the manager is able to add value. For example, the manager's hit ratio is 60% if the manager has 60 months of positive alphas and 40 months of negative alphas.

We can interpret the hit ratio as a measure of the frequency of success, rather than the degree of success. For instance, only a 100% hit ratio can guarantee that the manager is able to add value, for some hits are always more important than others. Although it may seem unlikely, even a 99% hit ratio can have negative overall alpha, if the negative alphas in the 1% cases are negative enough to offset all the small positive alphas in the 99% cases. Similarly, a manager with a low hit ratio, say, 30%, may be able to add value if the magnitude of the positive alphas is great enough. For instance, positive carry trades in bonds and currencies, and many option-writing strategies involve small gains most of the time, but occasional huge losses due to, for example, devaluation or default.[5] In other words, the hit ratio can tell us little about the profitability of the tactical strategy.

If alpha is symmetrically distributed, however, there exists a direct correspondence between the information ratio and the hit ratio. Assume alpha in each period follows a normal distribution with its mean the arithmetic average alpha, α_A, and its standard deviation the tracking error, TE. Then, we can express the hit ratio as

$$
\begin{aligned}
HR &= \Pr\left[\alpha_t \geq 0 | \alpha_t \sim N\left(\alpha_A, TE\right)\right] \\
&= \frac{1}{\sqrt{2\pi} \times TE} \int_0^\infty \exp\left[-\frac{1}{2}\left(\frac{\alpha_t - \alpha_A}{TE}\right)^2\right] d\alpha_t \quad (3.20)
\end{aligned}
$$

which can be reexpressed as

$$
HR = \frac{1}{\sqrt{2\pi}} \int_{-\frac{\alpha_A}{TE}}^\infty \exp\left[-\frac{1}{2}g^2\right] dg \quad (3.21)
$$

where $g = \frac{\alpha_t - \alpha_A}{TE}$. By definition, $\frac{\alpha_A}{TE}$ is the information ratio of the strategy. Therefore, the relationship between the hit ratio and the information ratio can be expressed as

$$
\begin{aligned}
HR &= \frac{1}{\sqrt{2\pi}} \int_{-IR}^\infty \exp\left[-\frac{1}{2}g^2\right] dg \\
&= \Pr\left[g \geq -IR | g \sim N\left(0, 1\right)\right] \quad (3.22)
\end{aligned}
$$

In words, if alpha is normally distributed, the hit ratio can be computed as the probability of obtaining a value greater than the negative of the information ratio under a standard normal distribution. Some examples of a monthly tactical trading strategy are tabulated in Table 3.1 .

Some may be surprised by the low hit ratios in the table, but to those with experience in asset allocation, the numbers should seem quite familiar. In Chapter 4, we see that for an unbiased tactical strategy of a single pairwise bet, such as between stocks and bonds, an annualized information ratio of 1.0 is considered truly exceptional. With such an outstanding performance, the

---

[5] Positive carry trades in bonds typically refer to those strategies with long positions in long-term bonds and short positions in short-term bonds. In currencies, positive carry means buying the currency with higher interest rate and selling the currency with lower interest rate.

Monthly IR	Annualized IR	Hit Ratio
0	0	50.0%
0.03	0.1	51.2%
0.06	0.2	52.3%
0.09	0.3	53.5%
0.12	0.4	54.6%
0.14	0.5	55.7%
0.17	0.6	56.9%
0.20	0.7	58.0%
0.23	0.8	59.1%
0.26	0.9	60.2%
0.29	1.0	61.4%

Table 3.1: Hit Ratio and Information Ratio with Normal Distribution

theoretical hit ratio, *if alpha is normally distributed*, is only slightly more than 60%. Even first-class asset allocation managers are expected to underperform 40% of the time. This may be the reason managers typically advise their clients that asset allocation strategies are expected to add value over a three- to five-year investment horizon, and that TAA is not suitable for everyone.

The relationship between the hit ratio and the information ratio for a broader range of values under a normal distribution is plotted in Figure 3.1.

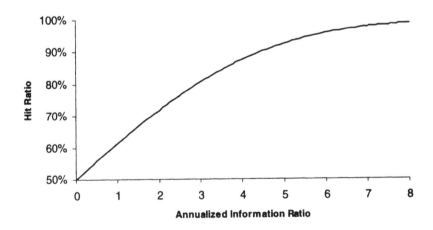

Figure 3.1: Hit Ratio and Information Ratio with Normal Distribution

3.6 Henriksson-Merton Test

Although it is less popular in the investment industry, the Henriksson-Merton (HM) measure of market timing ability is sometimes used as an additional evaluation criterion for tactical asset allocation managers. See Weigel (1991) and Philips, Rogers, and Capaldi (1996), for example. We describe here its conceptual underpinnings, implementation, statistical power, and relationship with other performance measures, besides some potential drawbacks and refinements.

3.6.1 Conceptual Underpinnings

Merton (1981) is a pioneer in application of the Black-Merton-Scholes option pricing model to interpret a market timing strategy as an option. To illustrate the concept, consider a simple pairwise decision between stock and bond. A manager with a perfect forecast of the future would have an end-of-period return equal to the maximum of the stock return and the bond return. That is:

$$R = \max\left[R_S, R_B\right] \tag{3.23}$$

An alternative strategy to get the same end-of-period return would be to hold a bond and buy a look-back call option on the return of the stock, with exercise price equal to the return of the bond.[6] If the stock outperforms the bond, the manager will exercise the option, paying the return from investment on the bond to exchange the return on the stock. If the bond outperforms the stock, the manager simply lets the option expire without exercising. The cost of this end-of-period return payoff pattern is obviously related to the premium of the option. As a result, one can use the option premium as a measure of the forecasting skill of the manager.

In deriving the theoretical framework, Merton first investigates selection of the future outperforming asset. For example, the manager attempts to predict which asset, the stock or the bond, is going to deliver the higher return in the following period. It is assumed that the manager does not attempt to predict by how much the stock will outperform the bond. The manager then adjusts portfolio positions in the stock and the bond.

Henriksson and Merton (1981) derive a non-parametric test for testing existence of market timing skill. To illustrate the concept, we again use the stock-bond pairwise bet example. One must first assume that only the sign of the stock return in excess of the bond return, $R_{S,t+1} - R_{B,t+1}$ (not its magnitude) conveys information about the probability that the forecast is correct. Define $p_1(t)$ as the probability of a correct forecast given $R_{S,t+1} > R_{B,t+1}$, and $p_2(t)$ as the probability of a correct forecast given $R_S < R_B$. Merton proves that for a forecast to have value, it must cause managers to adjust their prior beliefs about the probability distribution of future returns. Therefore, we can focus on the conditional probabilities in order to measure the skill of a manager. According

---

[6] Applying put-call parity, one can also show that the same end-of-period payoff can be obtained by a strategy using a put option.

to a theorem in Merton (1981), the necessary and sufficient condition for the
manager to modify prior beliefs is

$$p_1(t) + p_2(t) > 1 \qquad (3.24)$$

When the predicted and actual rankings of asset returns are independently
distributed, it implies that there is no market timing skill in the forecasts, and
$p_1(t) + p_2(t) = 1$. As a result, the HM test of market timing skill is equivalent
to testing the null hypothesis of

$$H_0 : p_1(t) + p_2(t) = 1 \qquad (3.25)$$

against the alternative hypothesis of

$$H_1 : p_1(t) + p_2(t) > 1 \qquad (3.26)$$

3.6.2   Implementation

To implement the HM test, the most direct and straightforward approach is to
construct a contingency table based on the forecasts and realized return. The
table can be constructed simply by counting the number of correct and incorrect
forecasts when the stock outperforms the bond, and vice versa. The most direct
approach is not necessarily the easiest approach, however.

An alternative implementation of the test is applied in Cumby and Modest
(1987) and Breen, Glosten, and Jagannathan (1989). The test requires estimating the regression:

$$I_t = a + bJ_{t+1} + u_t \qquad (3.27)$$

where I_t is 1 if the manager forecasts that the stock will outperform the bond
in period $t + 1$, and 0 otherwise; J_{t+1} is 1 if the stock does outperform the
bond in the period, and 0 otherwise; and u_t is an error term. The coefficient b
in the regression is an estimate of $p_1(t) + p_2(t) - 1$. That is, the HM test can
be implemented by first running the above regression, and then performing a
one-tailed test of $b > 0$.

3.6.3   Potential Drawbacks of HM Test

Although the HM test is based on the elegant option pricing theory, it has
some important limitations for applicability in the industry. While Cumby and
Modest show that when all the necessary assumptions of the HM test are valid,
it is indeed the uniformly most powerful unbiased test of market timing skill.
However, even with a sample size of one hundred, the test has uncomfortably
high Type II error for a low level of market timing skill. That is, the test has
inadequate power to reject the null hypothesis of no market timing skill when
in fact there is some. In reality, there are barely any tactical asset allocation
managers who have more than one hundred months of live performance. Consequently, the relatively weak power of the HM test in small to moderate sample
sizes will continue to limit its applicability.

Apart from its weak power, the test assumes that the conditional probability of a correct forecast is independent of the magnitude of subsequent returns. It treats realized returns as dichotomous variables. It is this critical assumption of the test that makes it an inappropriate test for many technical analyses, such as those using percentage filter rules, which clearly depend on the magnitude as well as the signs of returns.[7]

Furthermore, since only the probability, but not the degree, of being correct matters, it shares the same limitation of the hit ratio that it may not be informative about the profitability of a strategy. As we have noted, a strategy can be profitable even though it makes incorrect predictions more often than correct predictions. More incorrect forecasts than correct forecasts is an insufficient condition to rule out profitability.[8]

In short, because of its weak power and assumptions, the HM test is typically used in additional to other performance measures such as the information ratio as supportive statistics, instead of as the only evaluation measure.

3.6.4   Refined HM Test: Cumby-Modest Test

Cumby and Modest (CM) refined the original HM test by relaxing its assumption on independence of the conditional probability of correct forecasts and magnitudes of returns. In doing so, they find that the refined test can yield a very different conclusion on the presence of market timing skill. To implement the CM test, one need only estimate the regression

$$R_{S,t+1} - R_{B,t+1} = a' + b'I_t + u'_{t+1} \qquad (3.28)$$

where notations are defined as before. $b' > 0$ indicates positive market timing skill.

The major difference between the refined CM test and the original HM test is that the refined test also takes the magnitude of outperformance into consideration. By regressing the subsequent excess return of the stock over the bond on the manager's predicted ranks, the test measures not only how often the manager makes a correct forecast in a direction, but also how significantly one asset outperforms the other when it is predicted to be the better-return asset. By distinguishing small versus large market moves, the test takes into account the possibility that a manager may not add much value during flat or small market moves but may add value during volatile or large market move periods.

3.6.5   Potential Drawbacks of CM Test

While the CM test avoids treating realized returns as dichotomous variables, it has several potential drawbacks that continue to limit its application. The CM test in equation (3.28) considers only the mean, or first moment, of investment

---

[7] See Cumby and Modest for a more detailed discussion.

[8] This is equivalent to saying that the hit ratio is lower than 50%.

performance. It does not explicitly measure the variability of returns, which is an important performance measure that one should not ignore. In other words, it tells us little about the tracking error.

Furthermore, the way the CM test is specified in equation (3.28) assumes that the expected difference in stock and bond returns under the null hypothesis of no market timing skill, $H_0 : b' = 0$, is constant.

3.7   Applications of Performance Measures

We provide examples of application of the various performance measures to evaluate tactical asset allocation strategies. For ease of illustration, we focus on the pairwise decision between the S&P 500 and the 30-year U.S. Treasury bond. The strategy is assumed to be implemented monthly; at the end of each month, a tactical bet is made to shift the asset mix to the desired levels according to the signals. Because we use the arithmetic average for annualizing alpha and do not allow reinvestment of alphas into the portfolio, the performance measures are independent of the benchmark holdings as well as the degree of aggressiveness.

3.7.1   The "Low-Frequency" and "High-Frequency" Signals

Instead of running simulated signals, we use two signals developed specifically for the pairwise stock-bond decision. We denote these signals as "low-frequency (LF)" signal and "high-frequency (HF)" signal. The historical positions of the signals at the end of each month from December 1986 through March 1999 are plotted in Figure 3.2 and Figure 3.3.

It should be obvious from the figures that the LF signal does not change sign often, has a much longer wavelength, and is thus designed to capture the low-frequency pattern of the difference in stock and bond returns. In contrast, the HF signal changes sign more often, has a much shorter wavelength, and is designed to capture the high-frequency pattern of the difference in returns.

We have noted that most tactical signals have some degree of persistence such that the persistence is often preserved in their corresponding alphas as well. To further understand this point, one can start with the time-series dynamics of the signals. We estimate a simple time-series model, known as autoregressive moving average (ARMA) model, for each signal.[9]

The general form of an ARMA(p, q) model can be represented by

$$x_t = a + \sum_{i=1}^{p} \beta_i x_{t-i} + \sum_{j=1}^{q} \gamma_j \varepsilon_{t-j} + \varepsilon_t \qquad (3.29)$$

where p is the order of the autoregressive component; q is the order of the moving average component; and a, β_i, and γ_j are coefficients to be estimated.

---

[9] See Hamilton (1994) for detailed treatment of time-series models.

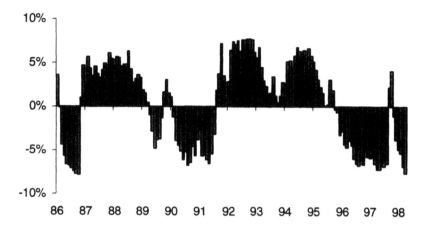

Figure 3.2: End-of-Month Low-Frequency Signal

The fitted models for the LF and HF signals are:

$$x_{LF,t} = -0.07 + 0.88 x_{LF,t-1} + 0.40 \varepsilon_{LF,t-1} + \varepsilon_{LF,t-1} \qquad (3.30)$$

and

$$x_{HF,t} = 0.35 + 0.34 x_{HF,t-1} + 0.35 \varepsilon_{HF,t-1} + \varepsilon_{HF,t-1} \qquad (3.31)$$

The estimates suggest that both the LF and HF signals can be characterized as an ARMA(1, 1) model.

In general, the degree of persistence of an ARMA process is indicated by the coefficients of the autoregressive components. Consistent with the patterns of the signals, the estimated models suggest that the LF signal, with an AR1 coefficient of 0.88, is much more persistent than the HF signal, which has an AR1 coefficient of 0.34. Nevertheless, we have verified that both signals have positive serial dependence and, therefore, according to equation (3.15), annualized tracking errors underestimate the degree of dispersion of annual alphas. As a result, annualized information ratios overstate the true performance.

3.7.2   Performance Measures of the Signals

The various performance measures of the two signals are summarized in Table 3.2.

Once again, the annualized alphas, tracking errors, and information ratios are independent of the benchmark, while the information ratios are independent of the degree of aggressiveness as well. As a result, we calibrate the scale of each

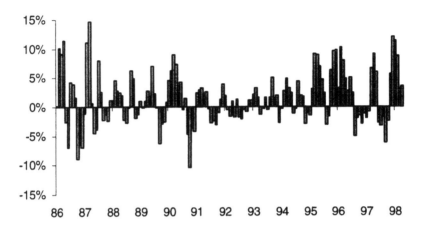

Figure 3.3: End-of-Month High-Frequency Signal

signal so that their tracking errors in the sample period are both 1% for ease of comparison. For an annualized tracking error of 1%, the LF signal returns an annualized alpha of 0.32%, giving an annualized information ratio of 0.32. For the same level of annualized tracking error, the HF signal delivers an annualized alpha of 0.80% and, therefore, a higher annualized information ratio of 0.80.

The hit ratio of the LF signal is 53%, comparing to the theoretical value of 53.5% in Table 3.1, when alpha is normally distributed. The hit ratio of the HF signal is 58%, compared to the theoretical value of 59%. To shed more light on the statistical distributions of alphas, we also perform statistical tests on the presence of excessive skewness and kurtosis.[10] Both test statistics suggest rejection of the null hypothesis that the alphas are normally distributed. Nevertheless, the theoretical hit ratios derived under normal distribution assumptions seem to be good approximations to the actual hit ratios in these two particular cases.

Finally, we implement both the HM test and the CM test for the signals. The results of the HM tests indicate that since $b > 0$ for both signals, both convey positive market timing information, which is consistent with hit ratios of over 50%. The information of the HF signal is statistically significant; the LF signal is not. The conclusions on the relative performance of the signals are consistent with their information ratios and hit ratios as well. Since there are more than twelve years of observations in the sample period, the weak power of the HM test may not be a concern here.

---

[10] A normal distribution has zero skewness and kurtosis of 3.0. The skewness and kurtosis formulas and the test statistics are from Kendall and Stuart (1977).

	LF Signal	HF Signal
Annualized Alpha	0.32%	0.80%
Annualized TE	1.00%	1.00%
Annualized IR	0.32	0.80
Hit Ratio	53%	58%
$H_0 : Skewness\ of\ Alpha = 0$	$p-value = 0.00$	$p-value = 0.00$
$H_0 : Kurtosis\ of\ Alpha = 3$	$p-value = 0.00$	$p-value = 0.00$
HM Test: one-tailed	$b = 0.0173$	$b = 0.1237$
	$p-value = 0.40$	$p-value = 0.02$
CM Test: one-tailed	$b' = 0.0035$	$b' = 0.0181$
	$p-value = 0.11$	$p-value = 0.03$

Table 3.2: Performance Measures of LF and HF Signals

The CM tests basically confirm the results of the HM tests, suggesting that both signals incorporate positive information, and the HF signal is a better-performing signal. An interesting observation is that the information of the LF signal comes closer to statistical significance, with a p-value of 0.11. Recall that the major difference between the HM test and the CM test is that the latter takes the magnitude of the stock-bond return difference into account. Therefore, the CM tests seem to imply that although the LF signal is less frequently correct, when it is right, the degree of outperformance or underperformance of stock is also higher.

Figures 3.4-3.7 plot monthly and rolling 12-month annualized alphas of both signals.

3.8 Concluding Remarks

We have discussed some commonly used performance measures for evaluating asset allocation managers. There is no one single measure that is sufficient for all purposes. We prefer to use annualized alpha, tracking error, and information ratio of the strategy. The hit ratio may also provide unique information, only when the normal distribution is a poor approximation of alphas. Both the Henriksson-Merton and Cumby-Modest measures have limitations. We choose not to include them in all subsequent empirical examples in this book.

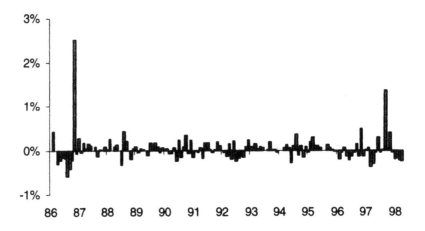

Figure 3.4: Monthly Alpha of Low-Frequency Signal

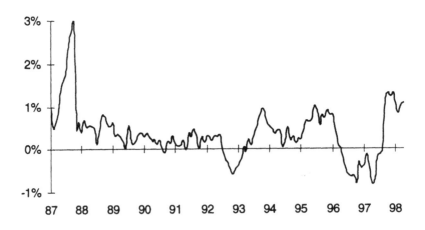

Figure 3.5: Rolling 12-Month Annualized Alpha of Low-Frequency Signal

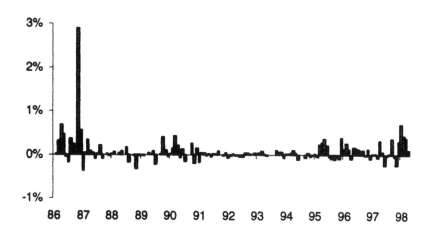

Figure 3.6: Monthly Alpha of High-Frequency Signal

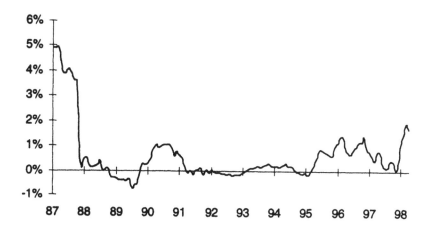

Figure 3.7: Rolling 12-Month Annualized Alpha of High-Frequency Signal

Chapter 4

Performance Characteristics Under Imperfect Information

4.1 Introduction

There are many arguments as to the determinants of alpha of tactical asset allocation. For example, Philips, Rogers, and Capaldi (1996) argue that it is the forecastability of asset returns. Sharpe (1987) argues that it is the contrarian nature of many tactical asset allocation strategies that captures the over-reaction of the markets. Probably motivated by the option-like interpretation of market timing proposed by Merton (1981), the asset allocation industry often links alpha to the variability of excess returns. For example, using actual trading results and simulations, Arnott and Miller (1997) argue that tactical asset allocation strategies can provide large profits only when there is substantial divergence in asset returns. The determinants of tracking error, however, are rarely studied and thus are less understood.

The objective of this chapter is to understand some commonly used performance characteristics of tactical asset allocation. In doing so, we use a pairwise asset allocation problem as a case study, and impose as little structure and assumptions as possible so that the results are general enough to be used as first-order approximations for all tactical asset allocation strategies. The approach we use can be modified to incorporate more structural assumptions, such as a time-varying covariance matrix, or multiple asset allocation decisions. We derive analytically tractable expressions for the average and variance of tactical bet, alpha, tracking error, and information ratio. To make our results more general and interesting, we allow the tactical bet to be biased. Furthermore, we illustrate the existence of a relationship between the information ratio and positive skewness in the return distribution. Finally, using our high-frequency signal for stock-bond asset allocation as an example, we illustrate how to use the analytical expressions.

4.2   Main Findings

We use a pairwise asset allocation between stocks and bonds as a case study. The equilibrium return of stocks is assumed to be higher than the equilibrium return of bonds so that the equilibrium risk premium is positive. We further assume a constant covariance matrix between stock and bond. This assumption can be relaxed, but only at the expense of more complicated derivations and less tractable expressions.

Tactical asset shifts are implemented by using liquid futures contracts, and therefore, transaction costs are negligible. While this same framework can be applied to other tactical strategies such as tactical duration management, currency management, style rotation, or sector rotation in different asset classes, transaction costs can become important when liquid futures contracts are not available.

The important findings are as follows:

1. An unbiased strategy should have a zero average tactical bet. A positive bias (overestimating the expected risk premium) leads to average over-weighting of stocks, while a negative bias (underestimating the expected risk premium) leads to average underweighting of stocks.

2. The variance of a tactical bet increases with the aggressiveness factor and the variance of the signal, but is independent of everything else.

3. There are two components of alpha:

   • A volatility capture component that increases with the information coefficient, volatility of signal, and volatility of risk premium; that is, it increases with the covariance of the current signal and the future risk premium.

   • A bias component that is positive (negative) if the bias is positive (negative).

4. The maximum allowable (negative) bias for the total alpha to remain positive is proportional to the square of the information coefficient and the square of the volatility-mean ratio of the risk premium.

5. Tracking error increases with the aggressiveness factor, the equilibrium risk premium, volatility of the risk premium, the information coefficient, and the volatility of the signal.

6. Under reasonable scenarios, the tracking error of a biased strategy is greater than the tracking error of an unbiased strategy, irrespective of the direction of bias.

7. The information ratio of an unbiased strategy is approximately equal to, but always lower than, the information coefficient.

8. The information ratio of an unbiased strategy increases with the information coefficient, but is independent of the aggressiveness factor.

9. The information ratio of an unbiased strategy can increase or decrease with equilibrium risk premium and the volatility of the risk premium, depending on the relationship between the two.

10. The optimal amount of bias to maximize the information ratio is approximately equal to the true equilibrium risk premium, and is thus independent of the level of skill (information coefficient) of the manager.

11. The information ratio of a positively biased strategy is higher than the unbiased information ratio, provided that the positive bias is not so large that it competes away limited tracking error from other signals, which leads to diminishing benefits from diversification of the tracking error.

12. The information ratio of a negatively biased strategy is always lower than the unbiased information ratio.

13. As long as the information coefficient is positive, returns distributions of an unbiased TAA strategy and a positively biased TAA strategy are positively skewed. For a negatively biased TAA strategy, the return can be either positively or negatively skewed, depending on magnitudes of the other parameters and the degree of negative bias.

4.3   Optimal Tactical Bet

We establish the case study by assuming that the future risk premium, y_{t+1}, can be predicted by a signal, x_t, which is available at time period t when the prediction is made, according to the linear relationship

$$y_{t+1} = a + bx_t + \varepsilon_{t+1} \tag{4.1}$$

which implies that the equilibrium risk premium μ_y and the equilibrium value of the signal μ_x are related by

$$\mu_y = a + b\mu_x \tag{4.2}$$

and the coefficient b is given by

$$
\begin{aligned}
b &= \frac{\sigma_{xy}}{\sigma_x^2} \\
&= \rho \frac{\sigma_y}{\sigma_x} \tag{4.3}
\end{aligned}
$$

where σ_{xy} is the covariance of x_t and y_{t+1}, ρ is the correlation between x_t and y_{t+1}, and σ_x and σ_y are the volatilities of x and y, respectively. The signal x_t

can be just one particular variable, or it can be interpreted as the composite information set used by the manager to predict the future risk premium. Focusing on the excess return of one asset over another is consistent with the pairwise bet structure discussed in Chapter 2.[1]

The information set must include only current and past information and is thus available at the time of prediction and implementation of the tactical bet. If the signal is simply the manager's expected risk premium, then the strategy is unbiased only when $a = 0$ and $b = 1$. In these specifications, the quality of information is measured by the correlation between the current signal and the future risk premium, that is, ρ. It is also commonly known as the information coefficient, IC.

Recall the results from Chapter 2 that when the investor's objective function is characterized by the mean and variance of the portfolio, the exante mean-variance-efficient optimal portfolio consists of three components:

- A global minimum-variance portfolio of stocks and bonds.

- A strategic bet on the equilibrium excess return.

- A tactical bet on the deviation of expected excess return from equilibrium.

When applied to the specifications above, this implies that the asset allocation manager should overweight stock only when the expected future risk premium is higher than the equilibrium risk premium. Similarly, stock is underweighted only when the expected future risk premium is lower than the equilibrium risk premium. Therefore, the optimal tactical bet is given by

$$Bet_t = F' \left[E[y_{t+1}] - \mu_y \right] \tag{4.4}$$

where F' is an aggressiveness factor applied to the risk premium, and $E[\cdot]$ is the expectations operator, which is understood to be formed at time t for the future risk premium at time $t+1$. Theoretically, F' is a function of relative risk tolerance and the variance of the risk premium, which are both assumed to be constant. In fact, the exact functional form for F' has been derived in Chapter 2, equation (2.21). In the simple case with two assets, its functional form is, according to equation (2.24), given by

$$F' = \frac{1}{\gamma \sigma_y^2} \tag{4.5}$$

where γ is the relative risk aversion coefficient such that $\frac{1}{\gamma}$ denotes the relative risk tolerance.

The intuition is simple. For the same variance of risk premium, an investor with a higher degree of risk tolerance will make more aggressive bets. Similarly,

---

[1] In practice, we find it more effective to predict excess return of one asset over another instead of returns of all individual assets for the purpose of TAA. While there may exist many return factors for different assets, some components of common factors may be hedged away in pairwise excess returns. This makes the job more focused.

for the same degree of risk tolerance, a lower variance of risk premium implies lower risk and, therefore, the investor again should more aggressive bets as well.

Substituting the expected and equilibrium risk premium, we obtain

$$Bet_t = F'\left[(a + bx_t) - (a + b\mu_x)\right] \tag{4.6}$$

which can be rewritten as

$$Bet_t = F\left[x_t - \mu_x\right] \tag{4.7}$$

where $F = F'b$ is a redefined aggressiveness factor applied to the signal instead. That is, when the current signal is above its average, we overweight stock. When the current signal is below its average, we underweight stock.

It is difficult to imagine, however, that the manager has perfect knowledge of the exact relationship between the future risk premium and the current signal. A bias can thus easily occur. For example, a bias can arise whenever any of the parameters (a, b, or both) in equation (4.1) is estimated with error, or when the manager makes a mistake in estimating the equilibrium risk premium, or the average signal.

To understand the effect of imperfect information on the performance of the strategy, we assume that the manager's view is biased so that the tactical bet is determined according to a linear investment rule instead:

$$Bet_t = F\left[(a + bx_t + \delta) - (a + b\mu_x)\right] = Fb\left[(x_t - \mu_x) + \left(\frac{\delta}{b}\right)\right] \tag{4.8}$$

Or:

$$Bet_t = F\left[(x_t - \mu_x) + \left(\frac{\delta}{b}\right)\right] \tag{4.9}$$

where δ is a bias in the expected risk premium. Again, this bias can come from any of the sources mentioned above, or it can be interpreted as a total bias from different sources. The fact that δ appears in the equation with b as the denominator is simply for scaling reasons. It is easy to see that a bias of $\frac{\delta}{b}$ in signal x is equivalent to a bias of δ in the expected risk premium y.

Throughout this chapter, we assume that there is no relationship between the bias and the signal. In other words, the bias is assumed to be exogenous. This assumption is violated when, for example, x depends on the equilibrium assumptions. In this case, the effect of the bias on the asset allocation performance becomes more complicated through its interactions with the signal as well as with the perceived expected risk premium. Unless we fully specify these interaction effects, it is not a well-defined problem. We choose to analyze a simplified case with an exogenous bias instead.

4.4 Performance Characteristics

By definition, alpha is equal simply to the product of the tactical bet and the subsequent realized one-period return of stock in excess of bond. That is,

$$\alpha_{t+1} = Bet_t y_{t+1} = F\left[(x_t - \mu_x) + \left(\frac{\delta}{b}\right)\right] y_{t+1} \tag{4.10}$$

We now turn to evaluating the performance measures of the strategy. Derivations of the analytical expressions listed below can be found in the Appendix.

4.4.1   Average Tactical Bet

The average tactical bet over a given period of time is given by

$$E[Bet] = F\left(\frac{\delta}{b}\right) = F\left(\frac{\sigma_x}{\rho\sigma_y}\delta\right) \tag{4.11}$$

It is intuitive to see that when the strategy is unbiased, the average tactical bet over a sufficiently long period of time has to be zero. For an unbiased strategy, the average expected risk premium measured over a long enough horizon has to be equal to the equilibrium risk premium. As a result, on the average, the tactical strategy should not overweight or underweight any asset. Equation (4.11), however, suggests that the strategy will have an average overweighting of the asset with higher average return when the bias is positive, and an average underweighting of the higher return asset when the bias is negative. Again, the result is intuitive, as a positive bias implies overestimation of future risk premium, and vice versa.

4.4.2   Variance of the Tactical Bet

The variance of the tactical bet is given by

$$Var[Bet_t] = F^2 \sigma_x^2 \tag{4.12}$$

Equation (4.12) justifies the intuition that the variance of the tactical bet increases with the aggressiveness factor and the variance of the signal. A more aggressive strategy will lead to more frequent and larger bets, while a volatile signal implies a higher volatility of tactical bets for the same degree of aggressiveness.

Note that it is possible that the volatility of the signal is a function of the volatility of risk premium. Some obvious examples include valuation signals and momentum signals, which clearly depend on price and return dynamics. As the risk premium becomes more volatilie, so do the signals.

4.4.3   Total Alpha

The total alpha of a tactical strategy is given by

$$E[\alpha] = F\left[\rho\sigma_x\sigma_y + \mu_y\left(\frac{\delta}{b}\right)\right] = F\left[\rho\sigma_x\sigma_y + \frac{\mu_y\sigma_x}{\rho\sigma_y}\delta\right] \tag{4.13}$$

Equation (4.13) provides some interesting insights into understanding the total alpha of a tactical strategy. It is found that there are two components in the total alpha of a tactical strategy.

Component 1: Alpha of Volatility Capture

The first component is the "alpha of volatility capture," denoted as α_{vc}:

$$E\left[\alpha_{vc}\right] = F\rho\sigma_x\sigma_y \qquad (4.14)$$

Or:

$$\text{Alpha of Volatility Capture}$$
$$= \quad \text{Aggressiveness factor} \times \text{Covariance}(\text{Signal, Risk Premium}) \quad (4.15)$$

It is equal to the product of the aggressiveness factor and the covariance of the current signal and the future risk premium.[2] This component obviously increases with the aggressiveness factor. As long as the signal has some information, the alpha of volatility capture can be increased simply by increasing the degree of aggressiveness until some benchmark constraints are reached.

Recall that the covariance of the current signal and the future risk premium is equal to the product of the correlation coefficient, the volatility of the signal, and the volatility of the risk premium. If the correlation of the current signal and the future risk premium, known as the information coefficient, is interpreted as the "quality of information," volatilities of the signal and the risk premium may be interpreted as the "quantity of information." This result seems to suggest not only that a good signal has high correlation with future risk premium, but that it must also be volatile enough such that more frequent and larger bets are taken for the same degree of aggressiveness. (We later establish that the volatility of the signal has absolutely no effect on the information ratio.)

When the volatility of the risk premium is high, there are more opportunities to add value, thus leading to a higher alpha. This is precisely the point made by Arnott and Miller (1997) on "substantial divergence in asset class returns." Our results provide a rigorous justification and quantification of this observation.

Since different tactical asset allocation managers will certainly have different signals, one cannot draw much inference on the alpha of volatility capture from the volatility of the signal. Our results do allow us to conclude that periods with low volatility of risk premiums are also tough periods for tactical strategies to add value. The most direct way to test our conclusion might seem to be by plotting some measure of average performance of a sample of tactical asset allocation managers.

Unfortunately, there are two problems associated with this test. First, not many asset allocation managers have a track record of more than ten years. This can make evaluation of performance difficult. If stock-bond relative performance is somehow associated with the business cycle, recent experience of the economy

---

[2] Granito (1987) illustrates how volatility capture works in duration averaging.

of the United States suggests that a ten-year period may be just barely enough to cover one full cycle. Second, our results, to be articulated next, suggest that the manager can add value simply by overweighting stocks to some extent. This second component of alpha can be difficult to separate from the total alpha.

To shed more light on this point, we plot the volatility of stock-bond excess returns over time since 1980. As there is no standard way of measuring volatility, we simply compute the 12-month rolling standard deviation of monthly stock-bond excess return. For consistency, we measure stock return by the total return of S&P 500, while bond return is the total return on the 30-year Treasury bond. The series is plotted in Figure 4.1.

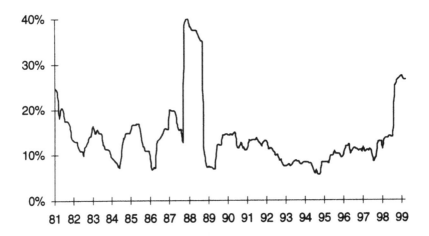

Figure 4.1: Rolling 12-Month Annualized Standard Deviation of Monthly Risk Premium

It is obvious that the volatility of the risk premium in most of the 1990s was near historical lows in the last two decades. The volatility rebounded substantially after the global stock correction in August 1998, but it is nowhere near its peak during the October 1987 global stock crash. Another interesting observation is the quick drop in volatility from its peak in 1987 to a low during mid-1989. Our theoretical results predict that it would be very difficult for tactical managers to add value during these periods of low volatilities. These predictions are consistent with the actual performance of tactical managers documented in Philips, Rogers, and Capaldi (1996).

In addition, if the volatility of the signal is somewhat proportional to the volatility of the risk premium, the dependence of alpha of volatility capture on the volatility of the risk premium can be stronger than what equation (4.14) appears to suggest. For example, if the volatility of the signal is a linear function of the the volatility of the risk premium, the alpha of volatility capture will be a function of the variance of the risk premium. This makes periods of low volatility of risk premium particularly difficult for TAA managers.

Component 2: Alpha of Bias

The second component is the "alpha of bias," which is given by

$$E\left[\alpha_{bias}\right] = F\left(\frac{\mu_y \sigma_x}{\rho \sigma_y}\delta\right) \tag{4.16}$$

When the bias is positive so that the strategy overweights stock on the average, the alpha of the bias is positive. Similarly, when the bias is negative so that the strategy underweights stock on the average, this component is negative. Its functional form suggests that the bias will have a greater effect on the total alpha when the information coefficient and the volatility-mean ratio of the risk premium are low, and when the volatility of the signal is high.

To illustrate the effect of a bias, we run a simple experiment by simply overweighting stock by 5% all the time from January 1987 through March 1999. The total annualized alpha of this "strategy" is 0.43%, with an annualized tracking error of 0.82%, giving an annualized information ratio of 0.52 and a hit ratio of 63%. Since the volatility of this "signal" is zero, the total alpha must be equal to the alpha of the bias. We plot the rolling 12-month annualized alpha of this constant positive bias of 5% in Figure 4.2.

Figure 4.2: Rolling 12-Month Annualized Alpha of a 5% Structural Stock-Bond Bet

Maximum Allowable Bias

We have shown that the total alpha of the strategy is the sum of the two components. From equation (4.13), we can infer that the total alpha remains positive if

$$\alpha > 0 \Leftrightarrow \delta > - \left(\frac{\rho^2 \sigma_y^2}{\mu_y^2} \right) \mu_y \tag{4.17}$$

If the bias is positive so that the strategy overweights stock on the average, the bias actually works in our favor, and it delivers a higher total alpha than the unbiased strategy. When the bias is negative so that the strategy underweights stock on the average, the strategy will still be able to deliver a positive total alpha as long as the inequality in equation (4.17) holds so that the positive alpha of volatility capture is greater in magnitude than the negative alpha of bias due to the average underweighting of stock. To give an example, assuming that the information coefficient is 0.2, with a volatility-mean ratio of risk premium of 10, equation (4.17) suggests that the total alpha will be negative only when the bias is negative and is greater than $4\mu_y$ in magnitude.

In addition, the maximum allowable bias is proportional to the square of the information coefficient and the square of the volatility-mean ratio of the risk premium. As a result, a relatively small improvement in the information coefficient can allow for a much more negative bias for the total alpha to remain positive. For example, if there is a 10% improvement in the quality of information so that the information coefficient is now 0.22, the total alpha will remain positive as long as the bias is not more negative than $4.84\mu_y$, a 21% increase over the original $4\mu_y$.

In practice, it is difficult to verify whether a strategy is biased or not. If the strategy has been implemented long enough so that at least one full cycle of relative valuation convergence of stocks and bonds has been observed, the average tactical bet may be used as an indicator of the absence of bias. If the strategy has a large positive average tactical bet on stock, it may imply that the strategy is positively biased, and thus, the manager's reported total alpha overstates the true level of skill of asset allocation.

4.4.4   Tracking Error

Tracking error, defined as the standard deviation of the total alpha, is given by the expression:

$$TE = F\sigma_x \sqrt{\left[(1 + \rho^2) \sigma_y^2 + \mu_y^2 \right] + \left[\frac{1}{\rho^2} \delta^2 + 2\mu_y \delta \right]} \tag{4.18}$$

Equation (4.18) for tracking error is a bit forbidding, and the existence of a bias further complicates the result due to some interactions with the equilibrium value and variance of the risk premium. To see the insights behind the mathematics, we first analyze the unbiased case, and then the more complicated case of a bias.

Unbiased Strategy

For an unbiased strategy that $\delta = 0$, it is easy to see that tracking error increases with the aggressiveness factor, the equilibrium risk premium, the correlation of the current signal and the future risk premium, the volatility of the signal and the volatility of the risk premium. A more aggressive strategy and a more volatile signal will both give rise to more frequent and sizable tactical bets, which, in turn, lead to higher tracking error. As alpha in each period certainly depends on the statistical distribution of the risk premium, the mean and variance of the risk premium thus enter into the expression for tracking error as well.

It is interesting to see that tracking error increases with the quality of information, just like the total alpha. As the quality of information of the signal is improved, tracking error of the strategy will also be higher. Since $-1 \le \rho \le +1$, it is straightforward to show that the tracking error of an unbiased strategy is bounded by

$$F\sigma_x\sqrt{[\sigma_y^2 + \mu_y^2]} \le TE_{\delta=0} \le F\sigma_x\sqrt{[2\sigma_y^2 + \mu_y^2]} \qquad (4.19)$$

As long as there is some information content in the signal so that $\rho \ne 0$, the tracking error will be higher than when we are trading on noise, i.e., $\rho = 0$, so that there is absolutely no information in the signal. Therefore, tracking error increases with the information content of the signal.

Biased Strategy

We can also demonstrate that the tracking error of a biased strategy is almost always greater than the tracking error of an unbiased strategy. If the bias is positive, $\delta > 0$, so that the strategy overweights stock on the average, the second bracket in the tracking error expression, $\left[\frac{1}{\rho^2}\delta^2 + 2\mu_y\delta\right]$, is always positive, implying that the positive bias always leads to higher tracking error. If the bias is negative, $\delta < 0$, so that the strategy underweights stock on the average, then the bias leads to a higher tracking error only when the second bracket remains positive, which is when

$$\delta < -2\rho^2\mu_y \qquad (4.20)$$

For example, if the information coefficient is 0.2, then a bias of only $-0.08\mu_y$ or lower is already enough to lead to a higher tracking error than the unbiased strategy. Therefore, under realistic situations, we can conclude that a biased strategy has higher tracking error than an unbiased strategy, irrespective of the direction of bias.

4.4.5 Information Ratio

Recall that the information ratio, IR, is defined as the ratio of alpha to tracking error. Using equations (4.13) and (4.18), the full expression of the information ratio is given by

$$IR = \frac{\rho\sigma_y + \frac{\mu_y}{\rho\sigma_y}\delta}{\sqrt{\left[(1+\rho^2)\sigma_y^2 + \mu_y^2\right] + \left[\frac{1}{\rho^2}\delta^2 + 2\mu_y\delta\right]}} \tag{4.21}$$

It is not easy to interpret this expression at first glance. Some interesting cases should make it more clear.

Unbiased Strategy

When the strategy is unbiased, it can be shown that the information ratio is simply

$$IR = \frac{\rho\sigma_y}{\sqrt{(1+\rho^2)\sigma_y^2 + \mu_y^2}} \tag{4.22}$$

Notice that since the aggressiveness factor and the volatility of the signal are common multipliers in both alpha and tracking error, they have zero net effect on the information ratio. For ease of interpretation, it is more convenient to express equation (4.22) as

$$IR = \frac{\rho}{\sqrt{1 + \rho^2 + \frac{\mu_y^2}{\sigma_y^2}}} \tag{4.23}$$

Or:

$$IR = \frac{\text{Inf. Coeff.}}{\sqrt{1 + (\text{Inf. Coeff.})^2 + (\text{Mean-Volatility Ratio of Risk Premium})^2}} \tag{4.24}$$

Since both the square of the information coefficient and the square of the mean-volatility ratio of the risk premium are positive but small in magnitude, it becomes obvious that for an unbiased strategy:

$$IR < \rho \tag{4.25}$$

and

$$IR \approx \rho \tag{4.26}$$

That is, for an unbiased strategy, the information ratio is approximately equal to, although always less than, the information coefficient. Our results can then be used to form realistic expectations on TAA performance. For example, it is well known among quantitative researchers that it is extremely rare to get an R-square of higher than 0.10 in monthly regressions of risk premiums. This suggests that an information coefficient of about $\sqrt{0.10} \approx 0.32$ seems to be the realistic upper bound. This gives a monthly information ratio of about 0.31, or an annualized information ratio of 1.07 for the unbiased strategy with monthly μ_y of 0.3% and monthly σ_y of 4.0%. Note that the information ratio is slightly less than, but close to, the information coefficient.[3]

From equation (4.22), it is obvious that the information ratio of an unbiased strategy decreases with the equilibrium risk premium. The reasoning is as follows. Since the strategy is unbiased, it does not overweight either asset on average, so the alpha is independent of the equilibrium risk premium. However, the volatility of alpha clearly increases with the equilibrium risk premium, which dictates the ranges of the realized risk premium in each time period.

To see the effect of the volatility of the risk premium on the information ratio for an unbiased strategy, equation (4.23) implies that for an unbiased strategy:

$$\frac{\partial IR}{\partial \sigma_y} > 0 \tag{4.27}$$

That is, the information ratio increases with the volatility of the risk premium.

To show the effect of the information coefficient on the information ratio for an unbiased strategy, we can rewrite equation (4.22) as

$$IR = \frac{\sigma_y}{\sqrt{\left(\frac{1}{\rho^2} + 1\right)\sigma_y^2 + \frac{\mu_y^2}{\rho^2}}} \tag{4.28}$$

Thus, it is also obvious that for an unbiased strategy:

$$\frac{\partial IR}{\partial \rho} > 0 \tag{4.29}$$

That is, the information ratio increases with the information coefficient. This becomes obvious when one recalls that the information ratio can be approximated by the information coefficient.

Biased Strategy

Interpretations become much more complicated when the strategy is biased. The most important question is the effect of the bias on the information ratio. To shed some light on this issue, we use a combination of analytical derivation and numerical examples. Without showing all the calculus and algebra, we differentiate the information ratio, given as the ratio of alpha in equation (4.13) and tracking error in equation (4.18), with respect to the amount of bias, δ. The optimal amount of bias, denoted as δ^*, is solved by setting the derivative equal to zero. The solution is verified as the global maximum. We establish the

---

[3] Again, one needs to be aware of the implicit assumptions made in annualizing performance measures that are discussed in Chapter 3.

result that the optimal amount of bias that maximizes the information ratio is given by

$$\delta^* = \left[\frac{\left(\frac{\sigma_y}{\mu_y}\right)^2 + 1}{\left(\frac{\sigma_y}{\mu_y}\right)^2 - 1} \right] \mu_y > \mu_y \tag{4.30}$$

Since the square of the volatility-mean ratio of the risk premium is much greater than 1, equation (4.30) implies that the optimal amount of bias is slightly greater than, but approximately equal to, the true equilibrium risk premium:

$$\delta^* \approx \mu_y \tag{4.31}$$

The optimal average tactical bet can then be determined in accordance with equation (4.11). Recall the definition that $F = F'b$, equation (4.11) suggests that the optimal average tactical bet to maximize the information ratio is approximately equal to $F'\mu_y$. For example, if F' is calibrated as equal to 3 with respect to a particular target tracking error, then for an equilibrium risk premium of, say, 3%, a positive bias of $3 \times 3\% = 9\%$ will be optimal.

Since δ^* is the global optimum, and the information ratio can be shown to be a concave function of the bias, it is easy to see that a negative bias always leads to a lower information ratio than in the unbiased strategy. This occurs because a negatively biased strategy will certainly deliver a lower alpha, while it almost always lead to a higher tracking error. As a consequence, *a negative bias is one thing that asset allocation managers should avoid at all cost.*

Although it is true that a positive bias will most likely lead to a higher information ratio, an extremely large positive bias can lead to a lower information ratio instead. Given the functional form of the information ratio and bias, this point can easily be proved mathematically. Intuitively, however, this result can be interpreted as follows.

Note that a bias, positive or negative, has absolutely no information about the future risk premium at all. As we have shown that a bias of realistic magnitude will always lead to higher tracking error, one can interpret that the bias actually introduces competition of tracking error from the signal that has positive information content.

Imagine that there is a fixed pool of tracking error that the strategy can consume. Although a positive bias always adds value, when it becomes so large that the marginal alpha it adds by taking some tracking error away from the signal is less than the marginal alpha lost from the signal, the net effect is a decrease in the overall information ratio. Alternatively, when the bias is so large that it becomes the dominating consumer of the limited tracking error, the benefits from diversification of tracking error diminish, which leads to a lower information ratio.

The exact cutoff point of this maximum allowable bias depends on other parameters of the strategy. Analytically, it can be solved by equating the general expression of the information ratio in equation (4.21) with the unbiased information ratio in equation (4.22).

To illustrate, Figure 4.3 plots the annualized information ratio as a function of bias, which is expressed as a multiple of the true equilibrium risk premium. We assume a monthly μ_y of 0.35%, monthly σ_y of 4.0%, and ρ of 0.2, which are close to historical sample statistics for monthly stock-bond premiums. This set of assumptions implies an annualized information ratio of 0.3 for a structural bet for stock (analyzed in detail in Chapter 6). The information ratio of the unbiased strategy, computed as 0.68, is depicted by the horizontal line in the figure.

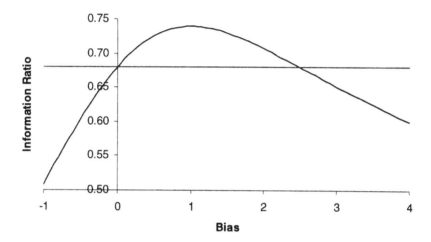

Figure 4.3: Annualized Information Ratio versus Bias in Multiples of Equilibrium Risk Premium

Consistent with the theoretical results, the information ratio of a strategy with zero bias is 0.68, the same as the unbiased strategy. As predicted by the theory, a negative bias, irrespective of its magnitude, always leads to a lower information ratio. For a positive bias between zero and about 2.5, the resulting information ratio is higher than the unbiased information ratio. When the positive bias is larger than about 2.5 times the equilibrium risk premium, information ratios of the biased strategies are lower than that of the unbiased strategy. In fact, the information ratio of a positively biased strategy approaches the asymptote of 0.3, which is the information ratio of the structural bet. When the positive bias is unreasonably large, the bias becomes so dominating that the whole strategy will become a structural bet, and therefore its information ratio should be the same as that of the structural bet as well.

Positive bias is prevalent in many investment areas. In a case study in Chapter 6, we further analyze more details of a positive bias, what we call a structural bet, in a tactical strategy.

4.4.6   Hit Ratio

The hit ratio is defined as the number of periods with positive alphas divided by the total number of periods during which tactical bets are made. As noted in Chapter 3, the hit ratio may reveal little about the profitability of a strategy. If alpha is normally distributed, there is a nonlinear but fixed relationship between the information ratio and the hit ratio, so the hit ratio is redundant. If alpha is not normally distributed, and in the worst cases, is not well approximated by any parametric distributions, the hit ratio becomes an indicator of frequency of success but not of the degree of success, which is measured by the profitability of the strategy. Consequently, the hit ratio is more of an empirical attribute that cannot be analyzed easily.

4.4.7   Skewness

Whether the first two moments of returns, mean and variance, are sufficient for measuring performance has long been under debate. As a natural extension of the two-moment framework, the skewness of the return distribution is frequently measured and analyzed. It is often argued that when two return distributions have equal means and variances, at least some investors would prefer the one that has positive skewness. In other words, investors prefer higher mean and skewness, but are averse to variance. In a portfolio context, it is the coskewness of an asset with the portfolio that matters, just as it is the covariance but not the variance of the asset that matters in a mean-variance portfolio framework.

It is beyond the scope of this book to discuss higher-moment asset pricing theory.[4] One study that focuses on the potential effects of TAA on skewness is MacBeth and Emanuel (1993). Using signals of dividend yield, price-to-earnings ratio, and price-to-book ratio, the study finds that, although the returns from the TAA portfolios may not be statistically different from the benchmark portfolio in a mean-variance framework, it appears that the TAA portfolio generates some degree of positive skewness, which is preferred by some investors. A limitation of the MacBeth and Emanuel study is that the results can be sample-specific and signals-specific.

We derive analytically tractable expressions in relation to the skewness of return of a TAA portfolio. Recall that the skewness of a random variable, z, is defined as the ratio of the third central moment to the cube of the standard deviation. That is:

$$Sk(z) = \frac{E\left[z - E[z]\right]^3}{\sigma_z^3} \tag{4.32}$$

Since the sign of skewness is completely determined by the numerator, we focus on the third central moment instead so as to make the analysis more tractable. As the total return of the TAA portfolio is equal to the sum of the benchmark

---

[4]See Ingersoll (1987) for an excellent description of three-moment asset pricing framework. Recent studies on skewness and coskewness as attributes in asset pricing models include Harvey and Siddique (1999, 2000).

portfolio return and alpha in each period, the additional degree of skewness, if any, that the TAA strategy can bring is all from the skewness of alpha. Therefore, we shift our focus to the third central moment of alpha.

By definition, the third central moment of alpha is given by

$$E\left[Bet_{t-1}y_t - E\left[\alpha\right]\right]^3 \tag{4.33}$$

where all variables have been defined. Applying all the moments and cross-moments, and expanding and rearranging terms, we prove in the appendix that

$$\begin{aligned} &E\left[Bet_{t-1}y_t - E\left[\alpha\right]\right]^3 \tag{4.34}\\ =\ & 2\rho\sigma_{Bet}^3\sigma_y\left(3\sigma_y^2 + \rho^2\sigma_y^2 + 3\mu_y^2\right) + \left(E\left[Bet\right]\right)^2 \times A + E\left[Bet\right] \times B \end{aligned}$$

where $E\left[Bet\right]$ and σ_{Bet} are the average tactical bet and the standard deviation of the tactical bet given by equations (4.11) and (4.12), respectively. The exact expressions of A and B are given in the appendix, and it is shown that $A > 0$ and $B > 0$. A close look at each term in equation (4.34) reveals that both the first and the second terms are positive, while the third term can assume either sign depending on the sign of $E\left[Bet\right]$.

Consider the case of an unbiased signal such that $E\left[Bet\right] = 0$, according to equation (4.11). In this case, the second and the third terms are zero, so the third central moment is positive. When the signal is positively biased such that $E\left[Bet\right] > 0$, all three terms are positive such that the third central moment is positive. In the case of a negatively biased signal, the third term is negative, while the first two terms are positive. Therefore, depending on the magnitudes of other parameters, the third central moment can be positive or negative.

Putting all these results together, we have established that both an unbiased TAA portfolio and a positively biased TAA portfolio have positive skewness in their return distributions, as long as information coefficients are positive; that is, $\rho > 0$. Just as a negatively biased TAA strategy can have a negative alpha and information ratio even though the signals have positive information, if the negative bias is dominating, it is likely to observe negative skewness in its return distribution as well.

While skewness might seem to be another performance measure for evaluating a TAA strategy, the fact that there is a direct relationship between the information ratio and skewness, except for negatively biased strategies, may limit its potential uses. It is also more complicated to compute, and is still less well understood than mean and variance. Nevertheless, it may be meaningful to report skewness along with other performance measures so that explicit comparisons can be made, provided that skewness is perceived to be an important characteristic.

4.5   Case Study: High-Frequency Signal

To illustrate application of the analytical expressions, we analyze in detail performance of our "high-frequency" signal for U.S. stock-bond asset allocation decision. This is the same HF signal that we first discussed in Chapter 3. At the end of each month from December 1986 through March 1999, we make a bet according to the value of the signal. Total returns of stocks and long bonds are computed based on the S&P 500 and the 30-year Treasury bond. For ease of reference, we plot the HF signal again in Figure 4.4.

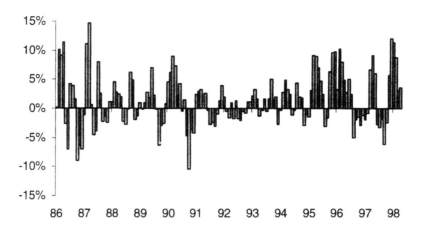

Figure 4.4: End-of-Month High-Frequency Signal

Notice that the signal is calibrated so that it gives a 1% tracking error in the whole sample period. As discussed in Chapter 3, the HF signal is designed to capture the high-frequency, short wavelength underlying the pattern of the stock-bond risk premium. As a result, it changes sign relatively frequently. According to the results in Chapter 3, the time-series dynamics of the HF signal can be characterized by an ARMA(1, 1) model as

$$x_{HF,t} = 0.35 + 0.34 x_{HF,t-1} + 0.35 \varepsilon_{HF,t-1} + \varepsilon_{HF,t} \tag{4.35}$$

so that it has some degree of positive serial dependence. Consequently, the annualized tracking error underestimates the true dispersion of annual alpha, while the annualized information ratio overstates the true annual information ratio.

Some statistical properties and performance characteristics of the signals and returns are tabulated in Table 4.1.

For a 1% annualized tracking error, the HF signal delivers an annualized alpha of 0.80%, giving an annualized information ratio of 0.80. Its hit ratio is 58%, implying that it has positive alphas 58% of the time, but negative alphas 42% of the time. In the whole sample period, the average bet is 1.51% for stock,

High-Frequency Signal	
Alpha	0.80%
TE	1.00%
IR	0.80
HR	58%
Average Bet: δ	1.51%
IC	0.26
Theoretical IR	0.94
Theoretical HR	60.5%

Table 4.1: Performance Statistics of High Frequency Signal

	HF Signal	Risk Premium	Alpha of HF
$H_0 : Skewness = 0$	$p - value = 0.09$	$p - value = 0.00$	$p - value = 0.00$
$H_0 : Kurtosis = 3$	$p - value = 0.67$	$p - value = 0.00$	$p - value = 0.00$

Table 4.2: Tests of Normality

which is denoted as δ in this chapter. The information coefficient is 0.26, which is computed as the correlation coefficient between the current HF signal and the subsequent realized monthly risk premium.

From these statistics, we compute the theoretical information ratio using equation (4.21) as 0.94. The theoretical hit ratio can then be determined to be 60.5% according to equation (3.22). There are apparently some discrepancies between actual and theoretical information ratios and hit ratios. As in all models, the underlying assumptions must be valid for the models to work as good approximations. Recall that almost all analytical expressions derived in this chapter are based on the assumptions that signals and returns follow a stationary, joint-normal distribution. Therefore, the discrepancies between theory and reality are likely due to violations of these assumptions.

To understand these discrepancies, we run some diagnostic tests on the statistical distributions of the HF signal, the monthly risk premium, and the monthly alpha of the signal. The results are reported in Table 4.2.

Focusing just on skewness and kurtosis, we find that the HF signal's violation of the normality assumption is not very significant. The only concern is that the HF signal may have some degree of skewness, which is indicated by a p-value of 0.09 for testing absence of skewness. The monthly risk premium is found to violate both the zero skewness condition and standard kurtosis for a normal distribution. As a result, the normal distribution can be a poor approximation for the alpha of the HF signal.

The reasons behind violation of normality of the monthly risk premium are unclear. It could be that the normal distribution is simply a bad approximation. Alternatively, even if the normal distribution is a good approximation, the parameters of the distribution may be time-varying so one may observe skewness and excessive kurtosis in a certain sample period of time.

Two common models are the jump-diffusion model and the stochastic volatilities model, but details on them are beyond the scope of this book.[5] We offer a visual inspection of the distributions instead. The frequency distributions of the HF signal, monthly risk premium, and monthly alpha of the HF signal are plotted in Figure 4.5, Figure 4.6, and Figure 4.7.

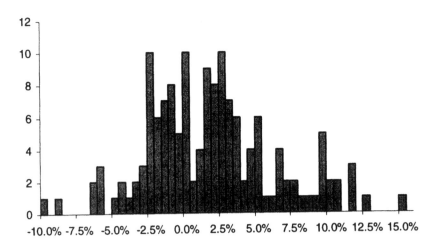

Figure 4.5: Frequency Distribution of High-Frequency Signal

4.6   Evaluating TAA Managers

The most interesting implication from equation (4.30) is that the optimal bias that maximizes the information ratio is independent of the level of skill, or information coefficient, of the manager, but is determined largely by the true equilibrium risk premium. These results have interesting implications for the evaluation of TAA performance as well as what TAA managers may do to increase their own information ratios.

In a simple world in which the stochastic processes for all assets and all state variables remain the same, all TAA managers, given their levels of skill, will attempt to maximize their information ratios simply by building in an intentional positive bias approximately equal to the true equilibrium risk premium. Since all managers are biased to begin with, the managers will, instead, build in a positive bias equal to their perceived equilibrium risk premium, i.e., $\mu_y + \delta$.

---

[5] See Das and Sundaram (1998) for examples and comparison of the two approaches.

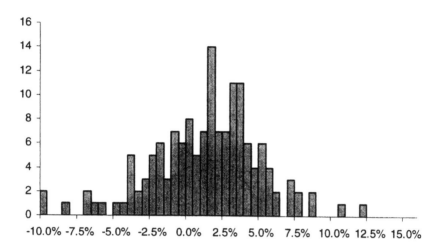

Figure 4.6: Frequency Distribution of Monthly Risk Premium

Consequently, together with the unintentional bias of δ, the total bias introduced to the strategy is $\mu_y + 2\delta$ under imperfect information.

In reality, all underlying processes, as well as managers' levels of skill, are likely to change. As a result, it is difficult to determine whether managers are overstating their true levels of skill by intentionally injecting a positive bias into their strategies. If a manager is found to have overweighted stock on the average in a reasonably long enough track record or backtest results, however, it is highly likely that there is a positive bias in the strategy, although we still cannot tell whether the bias is intentional or unintentional.

A simple example to illustrate the presence of a bias may be a particular type of momentum signal. Simple momentum signal, for example, is to buy the winner in the past three months and sell the loser in the last three months. Since stock offers a positive premium over bond, it would be more likely to be the past winner, and remain the winner in the future. As a result, although such a strategy may seem to do well, the signal itself can have little information content, and add value merely by sneaking in a positive bias for stock. Therefore, the total alpha of the strategy can be largely dominated by the alpha of bias.[6]

Alternatively, bias in inputs can also lead to bias in signals. It is well known that the earnings estimates of IBES are overly optimistic. If these estimates are used as inputs for a dividend discount model, the positive bias of earnings will

---

[6]The bias issue may exist in other investment areas as well. Conrad and Kaul (1998) analyze the sources of profits of a wide spectrum of return-based trading strategies implemented for stock picking. Their results suggest that the cross-sectional variation in the mean returns of individual securities included in momentum strategies (buy recent winners and sell recent losers) can potentially account for their profitabilities.

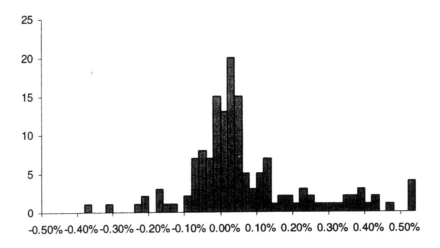

Figure 4.7: Frequency Distribution of Monthly Alpha of High-Frequency Signal

lead to a positive bias of the dividend discount rate, thus making stocks more attractive.[7]

Finally, when a positive bias equal to the perceived equilibrium risk premium is built in, according to equation (4.9), the optimal bet is to trade the expected risk premium, instead of its deviation from the perceived equilibrium. This implies that the asset allocation industry's definition of neutral stance is inconsistent with the objective of maximizing the information ratio. On the other hand, a TAA manager may be accused of playing a "strategic game" if the expected risk premium is traded, betting on the fact that the equilibrium risk premium is positive in addition to the manager's information advantage on the future risk premium.

In reality, it is not uncommon that some tactical managers simply compare their expected stock returns to cash returns in making a stock-cash bet, leading to a systematic overweight of stock, but are able to deliver good performance. Whether the current optimal tactical trading rule of equation (4.9), and thus

---

[7]Dividend discount model is the most important tool for valuation driven TAA managers in evaluating the attractiveness of stocks relative to bonds. Typically, the dividend discount rate is compared to the current bond yield. In the second half of 1990s, many valuation driven TAA managers underweighted stocks and have not done well due to the trending markets. Interestingly, one particular valuation driven TAA manager was able to deliver a positive alpha by substantially overweighting stocks. In 1998, this manager published a white paper in defense of her 12% - 13% dividend discount rate for S&P500, while most other managers had their dividend discount rates in the range of 7% to 9%. The main reason was because this manager used IBES earnings estimates. Although the resulting signal was highly correlated with signals of other valuation driven managers, its level was substantially higher than the others due to the positive bias in the earnings inputs.

the asset allocation industry's definition of neutral stance, should be changed depends on the objective of the managers, as well as whether the industry insists that trading the deviation of expected risk premium from its equilibrium remains the "rule of the game."

Nevertheless, a negative bias in the strategy should be taken seriously as a warning for both the manager and the client. A negative bias will always hurt performance after some period of time. Therefore, it seems to be reasonable to suggest that a strategy should be neutral on the average at worst. Still, some managers may choose to introduce a small positive bias as a hedge against business risk of underperformance, if not a large positive bias to play the strategic game.

4.7 Concluding Remarks

There are numerous approaches to estimate expected returns and risk premium in TAA strategies. To keep the theory as general as possible, we bypass the issue of what information should be used and how. Instead, we assume a linear relationship between the future risk premium and the signal, or set of signals, used by the manager. We generalize our results by introducing an exogenous bias in the expected risk premium. Based on these assumptions, we derive analytically tractable expressions for the average and volatility of tactical bet, alpha, tracking error, and thus information ratio, and skewness of portfolio returns. We also analyze the determinants as well as the effects of the bias on the information ratio. Since our results depend on only the most general assumptions, they serve as the first-order approximations for all TAA strategies.

Throughout the chapter, we assume that the frequency of trading is the same as the horizon of returns forecasting. That is, we assume that tactical trades are implemented once a month according to the expected monthly risk premium. In reality, TAA managers often implement tactical trades whenever a predetermined trigger is activated. Consequently, it is likely that these managers trade more frequently than the horizon of returns they attempt to forecast. In these cases, the results we have derived may need to be modified to incorporate potential effects of, for example, mean reversion in prices or relative prices so that the returns of different horizons do not have the same autocorrelation patterns. We leave this for future research.

4.8 Appendix

This appendix provides the derivations of the analytical expressions. We make significant use of moment-generating function (mgf) for univariate and bivariate normal distributions. To conserve space, we show only the resulting moments and cross-moments, which are to be used in the proofs.

To find the moments, we use the mgf of a univariate normal distribution for random variable Z:

$$M(z) = \exp\left(\mu z + \frac{\sigma^2 z^2}{2}\right)$$

The moment required is:

$$E\left[Z^2\right] = \frac{\partial^2 M(0)}{\partial z^2} = \mu^2 + \sigma^2 \tag{4.36}$$

To find the cross-moments, we use the mgf of a bivariate normal distribution for random variables z_1 and z_2:

$$M(z_1, z_2) = \exp\left(\mu_1 z_1 + \mu_2 z_2 + \frac{\sigma_1^2 z_1^2 + 2\rho\sigma_1\sigma_2 z_1 z_2 + \sigma_2^2 z_2^2}{2}\right) \tag{4.37}$$

The cross-moments required are:

$$
\begin{aligned}
E\left[Z_1 Z_2\right] &= \frac{\partial^2 M(0,0)}{\partial z_1 \partial z_2} \\
&= \mu_1\mu_2 + \rho\sigma_1\sigma_2
\end{aligned}
\tag{4.38}
$$

$$
\begin{aligned}
E\left[Z_1^2 Z_2\right] &= \frac{\partial^3 M(0,0)}{\partial z_1^2 \partial z_2} \\
&= \mu_1^2\mu_2 + 2\rho\mu_1\sigma_1\sigma_2 + \mu_2\sigma_1^2
\end{aligned}
\tag{4.39}
$$

$$
\begin{aligned}
E\left[Z_1^2 Z_2^2\right] &= \frac{\partial^4 M(0,0)}{\partial z_1^2 \partial z_2^2} \\
&= \mu_1^2\mu_2^2 + \mu_1^2\sigma_2^2 \\
&\quad + 4\rho\mu_1\mu_2\sigma_1\sigma_2 + 2\rho^2\sigma_1^2\sigma_2^2 + \mu_2^2\sigma_1^2 + \sigma_1^2\sigma_2^2
\end{aligned}
\tag{4.40}
$$

and

$$
\begin{aligned}
E\left[Z_1^3 Z_2^3\right] &= \frac{\partial^6 M(0,0)}{\partial z_1^3 \partial z_2^3} \\
&= 9\rho\sigma_1^3\sigma_2^3 + 6\rho^3\sigma_1^3\sigma_2^3 + 9\rho\sigma_1\sigma_2^3\mu_1^2 + 9\sigma_1^2\sigma_2^2\mu_1\mu_2 \\
&\quad + 18\rho^2\sigma_1^2\sigma_2^2\mu_1\mu_2 + 3\sigma_2^2\mu_1^3\mu_2 + 9\rho\sigma_1^3\sigma_2\mu_2^2 \\
&\quad + 9\rho\sigma_1\sigma_2\mu_1^2\mu_2^2 + 3\sigma_1^2\mu_1\mu_2^3 + \mu_1^3\mu_2^3
\end{aligned}
\tag{4.41}
$$

The proofs are as follows.
Proof of equation (4.11):

$$
\begin{aligned}
E\left[Bet_t\right] &= FE\left[(x_t - \mu_S) + \left(\frac{\delta}{b}\right)\right] \\
&= F\left(\frac{\delta}{b}\right)
\end{aligned}
$$

Proof of equation (4.12):

$$
\begin{aligned}
Var\,[Bet_t] &= F^2 Var\left[(x_t - \mu_S) + \left(\frac{\delta}{b}\right)\right] \\
&= F^2 Var\,[x_t] \\
&= F^2 \sigma_x^2
\end{aligned}
$$

Proof of equation (4.13):

$$
\begin{aligned}
E\,[\alpha] &= E\left[F\left((x_t - \mu_x) + \frac{\delta}{b}\right) y_{t+1}\right] \\
&= F\left\{E\,[x_t y_{t+1}] + \left(\frac{\delta}{b} - \mu_x\right) E\,[y_{t+1}]\right\} \\
&= F\left[\mu_x \mu_y + \rho \sigma_x \sigma_y + \left(\frac{\delta}{b} - \mu_x\right)\mu_y\right] \\
&= F\left[\rho \sigma_x \sigma_y + \mu_y\left(\frac{\delta}{b}\right)\right]
\end{aligned}
$$

Proof of equation (4.18):

$$
Var\,[\alpha] = E\,[\alpha_{t+1}^2] - E\,[\alpha_{t+1}]^2 \tag{4.42}
$$

$$
\begin{aligned}
E\,[\alpha_{t+1}^2] &= E\left[F^2\left((x_t - \mu_x) + \frac{\delta}{b}\right)^2 y_{t+1}^2\right] \\
&= F^2 E\left[x_t^2 y_{t+1}^2 - 2\left(\mu_x - \frac{\delta}{b}\right)x_t y_{t+1}^2 + \left(\mu_x - \frac{\delta}{b}\right)^2 y_{t+1}^2\right]
\end{aligned}
$$

Applying equations (4.36), (4.39), and (4.40), and rearranging terms:

$$
\begin{aligned}
E\,[\alpha_{t+1}^2] &= F^2\left[\mu_y^2 \sigma_x^2 + (1 + 2\rho^2)\,\sigma_x^2 \sigma_y^2\right] \tag{4.43} \\
&\quad + F^2\left[(\sigma_y^2 + \mu_y^2)\left(\frac{\delta}{b}\right)^2 + \frac{4\mu_y \rho \sigma_x \sigma_y}{b}\delta\right]
\end{aligned}
$$

Using equations (4.42), (4.13), and (4.43), and rearranging terms:

$$
\begin{aligned}
TE &= \sqrt{Var\,[\alpha]} \\
&= F\sqrt{[\mu_y^2 \sigma_x^2 + (1 + \rho^2)\,\sigma_x^2 \sigma_y^2] + \left[\sigma_y^2\left(\frac{\delta}{b}\right)^2 + 2\rho \sigma_x \sigma_y \mu_y\left(\frac{\delta}{b}\right)\right]} \\
&= F\sigma_x\sqrt{[(1 + \rho^2)\,\sigma_y^2 + \mu_y^2] + \left[\frac{1}{\rho^2}\delta^2 + 2\mu_y \delta\right]}
\end{aligned}
$$

Proof of equation (4.34):

$$E\left[Bet_{t-1}y_t - E\left[\alpha\right]\right]^3 \tag{4.44}$$
$$= \ E\left[Bet_{t-1}^3 y_t^3\right] - 3E\left[Bet_{t-1}^2 y_t^2\right]E\left[\alpha\right] + 3E\left[Bet_{t-1}y_t\right]E\left[\alpha\right]^2 + E\left[\alpha\right]^3$$

Equation (4.34) can then be derived by applying equations (4.38), (4.40), (4.41), and (4.13), combining and rearranging terms, where

$$A = 6\rho\sigma_{Bet}\sigma_y\left(1 + \sigma_y^2\right) > 0 \tag{4.45}$$

and

$$B = \mu_y\left(9\sigma_{Bet}^2\sigma_y^2 + 9\rho^2\sigma_{Bet}^2\sigma_y^2 + 3\sigma_y^2\mu_{Bet}^2 + 3\sigma_{Bet}^2\mu_y^2 + \mu_{Bet}^2\mu_y^2\right) > 0 \tag{4.46}$$

Chapter 5

Bias Therapy: Theory of Signal Filtering

5.1 Introduction

Moving averages have long been used in technical analysis for trading strategies. Typically, buy or sell decisions are triggered when the variable crosses its moving average from below or above. Some technical analysts, that is, see a change from a rising to a declining market when a price moves below its moving average; the movement of a price above the moving average is interpreted as bullish.

Moving averages are also widely used as proxies for changing equilibrium values. The difference between the current value of a variable and its moving average may be seen as a signal for tactical shifts between two asset classes. A large difference suggests relative bullishness for one asset, and a small difference suggests relative bearishness for one asset. There must, however, be a point of reference in place for one to judge whether the current difference is great or small. Different versions of moving averages are used for this purpose, including simple, weighted, and exponential moving averages. The intuition is obvious. If the equilibrium is indeed continually changing, its dynamics will be largely captured by the moving averages.

Equilibrium, however, is an unobservable state. Whether it is changing or not is likely to depend on the particular period. If the equilibrium is in fact stable, the use of moving averages will distort trading strategies. An alternative is simply to use a forward-looking equilibrium assumption instead. In terms of probability, it is unlikely to have a perfect specification of the unobservable equilibrium. Thus, a forward-looking assumption also introduces bias.

In Chapter 4, we analyze the effect of a bias on performance characteristics of a tactical strategy. Results suggest that while a reasonable amount of positive bias increases the information ratio, a negative bias always leads to a lower information ratio than the unbiased strategy. Bias can originate in imprecise estimation of parameters, including the equilibrium risk premium and the equilibrium values of the signals. A positive bias can be the result of underestimating equilibrium, while a negative bias can be the result of overestimating equilibrium.

In this chapter, we compare the costs and benefits of signal filtering with simple moving averages versus a forward-looking assumption of equilibrium specification when the true equilibrium is stable. Specifically, the value of a current signal relative to its moving average, and relative to the equilibrium value are used to trigger tactical shifts between two assets, say, stocks and bonds. More focus is given to the case of negative bias, which hurts performance. We demonstrate that bias in a signal will be removed when the signal-filtering strategy is implemented for a reasonably long period of time. The bias introduced by the forward-looking assumption remains, however, no matter the period of implementation.

We also establish the result that, with the signal-filtering strategy, it is actually the changes, not just the levels of the signal that trigger tactical shifts. Furthermore, we quantify the required accuracy for the forward-looking assumption to be a competitive alternative to the signal-filtering strategy. Under reasonable market conditions, we demonstrate in theory and with simulation that a biased strategy requires good quality information so that the alpha of volatility capture (the predictability of the future risk premium) is high enough to offset the negative alpha of bias. It is thus not as easy to outperform the signal-filtering strategy, which completely eliminates the negative alpha of bias, but at the expense of a lower alpha of volatility capture.

5.2   Bias in the Tactical Bet

A bias in equilibrium specification can be transformed into a bias in the tactical bet so that one asset is systematically overweighted. We also illustrate how the bias in the tactical bet can be removed when the signal is filtered.

We analyze a signal for stocks, x_S, and a signal for bonds, x_B. For example, x_S can be the dividend discount rate or the expected stock return, while x_B can be the bond yield or the expected bond return. For simplicity and tractability, assume that both signals follow a mean-reverting process with the same parameter for speed of mean reversion, k, as follows

$$x_{S,t} = (1 - k)\,\mu_S + kx_{S,t-1} + \varepsilon_{S,t} \tag{5.1}$$

and

$$x_{B,t} = (1 - k)\,\mu_B + kx_{B,t-1} + \varepsilon_{B,t} \tag{5.2}$$

such that the expected values of the signals at time $t+1$ based on the information available at time t are given by

$$E\left[x_{S,t+1}\right] = (1 - k)\,\mu_S + kx_{S,t} \tag{5.3}$$

and

$$E[x_{B,t+1}] = (1 - k) \mu_B + kx_{B,t} \tag{5.4}$$

where μ_S and μ_B are the true equilibrium values, and are assumed to be stable over time.

To introduce a bias into the system, we assume that the manager has a bias, δ, on the forward-looking equilibrium level of the stock signal, but has perfect knowledge of the stochastic process of the bond signal. That is, the manager perceives that the stock signal follows the stochastic process

$$x_{S,t} = (1 - k) (\mu_S + \delta) + kx_{S,t-1} + \varepsilon_{S,t} \tag{5.5}$$

and thus, a biased expected value of the stock signal is formed as

$$E^b [x_{S,t+1}] = (1 - k) (\mu_S + \delta) + kx_{S,t} \tag{5.6}$$

where the superscript b denotes that the expectation is biased.

According to the analysis in Chapter 4, the tactical bet is equal to an aggressiveness factor, F, times the deviation of the current difference of the signal from its equilibrium value. The deviation is thus used as the tactical signal. For simplicity and without loss of generality, we assume that F is equal to 1. Accordingly, the tactical bet based on the unbiased expectations is

$$\begin{aligned} Bet_t &= (E[x_{S,t+1}] - E[x_{B,t+1}]) - (\mu_S - \mu_B) \\ &= k[(x_{S,t} - x_{B,t}) - (\mu_S - \mu_B)] \end{aligned} \tag{5.7}$$

When expectations are biased, the tactical bet based on the biased signals becomes

$$\begin{aligned} Bet_t^b &= (E^b[x_{S,t+1}] - E[x_{B,t+1}]) - (\mu_S + \delta - \mu_B) \\ &= k[(x_{S,t} - x_{B,t}) - (\mu_S + \delta - \mu_B)] \end{aligned} \tag{5.8}$$

If the tactical asset allocation strategy is implemented for a sufficiently long period of time, the realized observations of the signals can provide unbiased estimates of their equilibrium values. That is, $E[x_S] = \mu_S$, and $E[x_B] = \mu_B$.

In this case, it is straightforward to show that

$$E[Bet_t] = 0 \tag{5.9}$$

That is, on the average, an unbiased strategy does not overweight either asset. Similarly, when expectations are biased, it can be shown that the average tactical bet is given by

$$E[Bet_t^b] = k\delta \tag{5.10}$$

The results suggest that a biased view can be transformed into a systematic average overweight or underweight of one asset, depending on the direction or sign of the bias.

According to the results of Chapter 4, the total alpha of a tactical strategy has two components:

$$\text{Total Alpha} = \text{Alpha of Volatility Capture} + \text{Alpha of Bias} \qquad (5.11)$$

We analyze in detail the effects of signal filtering with moving averages on each component of the total alpha. In general, we find that signal filtering reduces the alpha of volatility capture, because it does not make maximum use of all information, but it completely eliminates the alpha of bias. The net effect on the total alpha becomes a trade-off of the two.

5.3 Mitigating the Bias with Signal Filtering

We investigate the use of a simple moving average filter in an attempt to mitigate the effect of the bias. In particular, we study a moving average rule. Instead of subtracting the forward-looking equilibrium assumption from the difference of the current values of stock and bond signals, we subtract a simple moving average of past differences. That is,

$$Bet_t^f = \left(E^b\left[x_{S,t+1} \right] - E\left[x_{B,t+1} \right] \right) - \frac{1}{m} \sum_{i=1}^{m} \left(E^b\left[x_{S,t+1-i} \right] - E\left[x_{B,t+1-i} \right] \right)$$

$$(5.12)$$

where the superscript f indicates that the tactical bet is taken with the filtered signals, whether the view is biased or not, and m denotes the window length for computing the historical moving average. Substituting the expected values of the signals and rearranging, we have

$$Bet_t^f = k \left[x_{S,t} - x_{B,t} - \frac{1}{m} \sum_{i=1}^{m} \left(x_{S,t-i} - x_{B,t-i} \right) \right] \qquad (5.13)$$

As revealed in equation (5.13), after filtering by a simple moving average, the bias, δ, is eliminated from the tactical bet. If the statistical distributions of the signals are ergodic such that realized values at all time periods are drawn from the same distributions, it is obvious that

$$E\left[x_{S,t+i} \right] = \mu_S \qquad (5.14)$$

and

$$E\left[x_{B,t+i} \right] = \mu_B \qquad (5.15)$$

for all values of i. When a long enough history of data is available, so that the moving average window sweeps through ranges of variations in indicators, it becomes easy to show that

$$E\left[Bet_t^f \right] = 0 \qquad (5.16)$$

In other words, even if the forward-looking equilibrium assumptions are biased, the systematic overweight or underweight of one asset has been removed by the moving average filter.

5.4 Changes in Signal versus Levels of Signal

For purposes of illustration, assume that a signal available at current time t, x_t, can be used to predict the future value of another variable in the next period at $t+1$, y_{t+1}. In our example of stock-bond allocation, one may interpret x_t as the expected future risk premium, and y_{t+1} as the actual future risk premium that the manager is trying to predict. Again, similar to the discussion in previous chapters, x_t may represent an information set that includes many different variables, or it can be just one variable. We maintain the assumption that x_t follows a mean-reverting process with the speed of mean reversion denoted by k. Without loss of generality, the same functional form of equation (5.1) can be applied to x_t:

$$x_t = (1 - k)\,\mu_x + kx_{t-1} + \varepsilon_{x,t} \tag{5.17}$$

Applying the moving average filter, and ignoring the aggressiveness factor as well as the speed of mean reversion parameter, k, we can simply use equation (5.13) to show that the tactical bet is given by

$$Bet_t^f = x_t - \frac{1}{m}\sum_{i=1}^{m} x_{t-i} \tag{5.18}$$

Notice that the historical m-period moving average is used as if it were the equilibrium. For further insight into the filtered bet, we rewrite equation (5.18) as

$$
\begin{aligned}
Bet_t^f &= \frac{1}{m}\sum_{i=1}^{m}(x_t - x_{t-i}) \\
&= \frac{1}{m}\left[(x_t - x_{t-1}) + (x_t - x_{t-2}) + ... + (x_t - x_{t-m})\right]
\end{aligned}
\tag{5.19}
$$

Equation (5.19) reveals that the bet in a signal-filtering rule is in fact a bet on the simple average of the differences between the current value of the signal and its value in the past m periods. In general, all other versions of moving average rules can be interpreted in a similar fashion, but with different weights assigned to various past periods. Moreover, a simple differencing rule can also be interpreted as a special case of a signal-filtering rule. For example, a first-differencing rule is obtained by assigning all the weights to $x_t - x_{t-1}$, and zero weight to others. In this way, we can interpret the signal-filtering rule as one that uses changes in the signal, rather than just levels of the signal, to trigger a tactical shift.

In practice, a filter may be implicitly applied in many cases. For example, instead of simply referring to their current stance or their view of the stock market, many managers like to compare their changes in view over time, such as whether they are becoming "more bullish" or "more bearish." Thus, it is the changes in signal rather than the levels of signal that trigger a trade. Some

managers also like to compute "momentum" of their signals, basically by comparing the current values to the past values of the signals. Whether it is the first
difference, or the difference between current value and the value of the signal
one year ago, or other combinations, these can be analyzed as special cases of
equation (5.19). Our general results can be applied accordingly.

Analysts are frequently asked to indicate their forward-looking equilibrium
assumptions, such as for the equity risk premium, bond yields, inflation, growth,
and the like. When one cannot assure that these views are unbiased, our results
suggest that it may be worth considering changes in analyst assumptions as
well as the levels. In fact, some surveys report both current and past values of
analyst forecasts. Or analysts may be asked to submit changes in equilibria, as
well as the levels.

5.5   Effects of Signal Filtering on Information Ratio and Alpha of Volatility Capture

There are costs to using a moving average filter when the equilibrium is stable.
In this case, the signal-filtering rule introduces another source of bias, which
can adversely affect the quality of information. Recall from Chapter 4 that the
information coefficient is an important determinant of the alpha of volatility
capture. It is therefore of critical importance to understand how signal filtering
affects the performance of the strategy.

Let ρ be the information coefficient, that is, the correlation coefficient between the current signal and the future risk premium:

$$Corr(x_t, y_{t+1}) = \rho \qquad (5.20)$$

That is, ρ measures the quality of our information. The higher the information
coefficient, the better the signal is at predicting the future risk premium, and
the higher the quality of information. Since adding or subtracting a constant
only shifts the variable up or down by a level, this does not affect its degree
of correlation with another variable. We can therefore state without proof that
the information coefficient of the strategy using a forward-looking equilibrium
assumption is ρ, whether it is biased or not:

$$Corr\left(x_t - (\mu_x + \delta), y_{t+1}\right) = \rho \qquad (5.21)$$

where $(\mu_x + \delta)$ is the potentially biased forward-looking equilibrium assumption.
In other words, there is no loss of information in this strategy. This, however,
says little about the performance of the strategy, which also depends on the
alpha of bias. For instance, the total alpha of a negatively biased strategy can
be negative if the bias is sufficiently negative to offset the positive alpha of
volatility capture based on the quality of information.

An important question about the signal-filtering strategy relates to the correlation of the future risk premium and the filtered signal. That is, we attempt

to quantify $Corr\left(x_t - \frac{1}{m}\sum_{i=1}^{m}x_{t-i}, y_{t+1}\right)$. This is an important question, as it addresses the possibility and the extent of the distortion of information by signal filtering.

It is necessary first to impose some simplifying assumptions about the behavior of the signal. Again, we assume that the signal is mean-reverting so that it can be depicted at discrete time, t, as in equation (5.17), where $0 < k < 1$. The smaller the value of k, the faster the mean reversion, and the less persistent x.

To illustrate, we plot the first 500 observations of two simulated mean-reverting series with zero mean and standard deviation of 2% in Figure 5.1 and Figure 5.2 for values of k of 0.8 and 0.9. The series with $k = 0.8$ obviously crosses the mean at zero more often than the series with $k = 0.9$. It is thus said to be more mean-reverting, or less persistent, or having faster mean reversion.

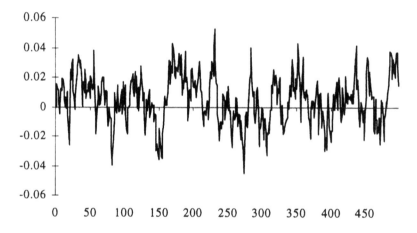

Figure 5.1: Mean-Reverting Process: k = 0.80

To analyze the degree of retention of information by signal filtering, we prove in the appendix that the information coefficient of the filtered signal is given by

$$Corr\left(x_t - \frac{1}{m}\sum_{i=1}^{m}x_{t-i}, y_{t+1}\right) = \theta\rho \tag{5.22}$$

where

$$\theta = \frac{1 - \frac{k}{m}\left(\frac{1-k^m}{1-k}\right)}{\sqrt{1 - \left(\frac{2km-1}{m^2}\right)\left(\frac{1-k^m}{1-k}\right) + \frac{1+k}{m^2}\left[\left(\frac{m-1}{1-k}\right) - \frac{k(1-k^{m-1})}{(1-k)^2}\right]}} \tag{5.23}$$

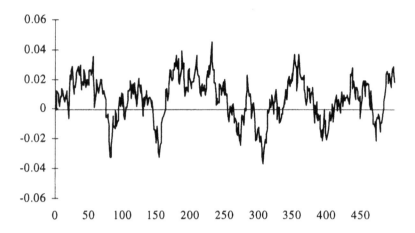

Figure 5.2: Mean-Reverting Process: k = 0.90

for any arbitrary $0 < k < 1$ and moving average window size, m.

Given this functional form, θ can be interpreted as the degree of information retention, given as the ratio of correlation of y_{t+1} with the filtered signal to the correlation of y_{t+1} with the original signal. The lower the value of θ, the more the information is lost through signal filtering. A θ of 1.00 implies that loss of information is insignificant.

As we illustrate later, it is the implications instead of the exact values of θ that are important to understand. To ensure the robustness of our results and implications, we simulate for several different values of k with different values of m in order to verify the validity of equation (5.23). The simulated results are close enough to the theoretical values based on the prespecified criterion, and the details are not reported here.

According to equations (5.22) and (5.23), the retention of information measured by the information coefficient depends on

1. The speed of mean reversion of the signal, k, and

2. The moving average window size, m.

Without giving all the details, it can be shown that $\theta < 1$ for all values of k and m. That is, we have established the result that

$$Corr\left(x_t - \frac{1}{m}\sum_{i=1}^{m} x_{t-i}, y_{t+1}\right) \quad < \quad Corr\left(x_t, y_{t+1}\right) \tag{5.24}$$

$$= \quad Corr\left(x_t - \left(\mu_X + \delta\right), y_{t+1}\right)$$

m	Speed of Mean Reversion Parameter: k									
Months	0.98	0.96	0.94	0.92	0.90	0.88	0.86	0.84	0.82	0.80
12	0.30	0.41	0.48	0.54	0.59	0.63	0.66	0.69	0.72	0.74
24	0.40	0.54	0.62	0.68	0.73	0.76	0.79	0.81	0.83	0.85
36	0.48	0.62	0.70	0.76	0.80	0.82	0.85	0.86	0.88	0.89
48	0.53	0.67	0.75	0.80	0.84	0.86	0.88	0.89	0.91	0.92
60	0.58	0.72	0.79	0.84	0.86	0.89	0.90	0.91	0.92	0.93
72	0.61	0.75	0.82	0.86	0.88	0.90	0.92	0.93	0.93	0.94
84	0.65	0.78	0.84	0.88	0.90	0.92	0.93	0.94	0.94	0.95
96	0.67	0.80	0.86	0.89	0.91	0.92	0.94	0.94	0.95	0.96
108	0.70	0.82	0.87	0.90	0.92	0.93	0.94	0.95	0.96	0.96
120	0.72	0.83	0.88	0.91	0.93	0.94	0.95	0.95	0.96	0.96

Table 5.1: Measure of Information Retention: Monthly Data

m	Speed of Mean Reversion Parameter: k									
Days	0.98	0.96	0.94	0.92	0.90	0.88	0.86	0.84	0.82	0.80
50	0.54	0.68	0.76	0.81	0.84	0.87	0.88	0.90	0.91	0.92
100	0.68	0.81	0.86	0.89	0.91	0.93	0.94	0.95	0.95	0.96
150	0.76	0.86	0.90	0.93	0.94	0.95	0.96	0.96	0.97	0.97
200	0.80	0.89	0.93	0.94	0.95	0.96	0.97	0.97	0.98	0.98
250	0.84	0.91	0.94	0.95	0.96	0.97	0.97	0.98	0.98	0.98
300	0.86	0.92	0.95	0.96	0.97	0.97	0.98	0.98	0.98	0.99
350	0.88	0.93	0.96	0.97	0.97	0.98	0.98	0.98	0.99	0.99
400	0.89	0.94	0.96	0.97	0.98	0.98	0.98	0.99	0.99	0.99
450	0.90	0.95	0.97	0.97	0.98	0.98	0.99	0.99	0.99	0.99
500	0.91	0.95	0.97	0.98	0.98	0.98	0.99	0.99	0.99	0.99

Table 5.2: Measure of Information Retention: Daily Data

This result suggests that signal filtering with moving averages to some extent throws away some information. Irrespective of the speed of mean reversion of the signal or the window size of the moving average filter, the quality of information of the filtered signal is always worse than the quality of information of the original signal.

To provide some examples, we report the theoretical values of θ for a range of speed of mean reversion parameters $0.80 \leq k \leq 0.98$ and a moving average window size ranging from one year (12 months) to ten years (120 months) in Table 5.1. Similarly, Table 5.2 reports the values of θ for daily data, with moving-average window size ranging from about two months (50 days) to two years (500 days).

It is necessary to emphasize that we assume that the stochastic process of x remains the same, with the same mean and the same speed of mean reversion during the period of interest. Regime shifts in means or other parameters of the statistical distributions are interesting, but beyond the scope of this book because of the degree of sophistication and less tractability.

Two important results emerge from the tables:

1. The slower the speed of mean reversion (large k), and/or

2. The smaller the moving average window size (small m),

the more the loss of information through signal filtering.

These results can be demonstrated using an example. Consider the very special case of $k = 1$ and $m = 1$. For $k = 1$, the signal follows a random walk so that there is absolutely no tendency for the signal to mean-revert. For $m = 1$, the filter is simply a first-differencing. Applying equation (5.17) with these values of k and m, it can easily be shown that the filtered signal is simply

$$x_t - x_{t-1} = \varepsilon_{x,t} \tag{5.25}$$

As shown in the above equation, the first difference of a random walk is random noise. Signal filtering in this case completely throws away all information.

Strictly speaking, Table 5.1 and Table 5.2 are not directly comparable. A monthly process is different from a daily process even when the speed of the mean reversion parameter is exactly the same. Nevertheless, it is apparent that there is much less loss of information through signal filtering with daily data than in the case of monthly data. The information coefficient is about 10% lower with a moderate speed of mean reversion (0.88) and moving average window size (72 months) with monthly data. In fact, with reasonable values of k and a moving average window size of two to three years, almost all information is retained using daily data.

These findings support a conclusion that the adverse effect of signal filtering with moving averages on the alpha of volatility capture is relatively small, or even insignificant when the conditions are more favorable.

5.6 Effects of Signal Filtering on Volatility of Tactical Bets

It is obvious that the signs of the bets based on the original and the filtered signals will not be the same in all periods. Consequently, it is not meaningful to compare the resulting bets in each period. Instead, we compare the volatilities of the tactical bets. In general, the more volatile the bets, the wider the range of the bets, and the more aggressive the strategy.

In the original strategy in which we simply bet on the difference of the current signal and the forward-looking equilibrium assumption, the variance of the bet is given by

$$\begin{aligned} Var(Bet) &= Var\left(x_t - (\mu_x + \delta)\right) \\ &= \sigma_x^2 \end{aligned} \tag{5.26}$$

m	Speed of Mean Reversion Parameter: k									
Months	0.98	0.96	0.94	0.92	0.90	0.88	0.86	0.84	0.82	0.80
12	0.41	0.55	0.65	0.72	0.78	0.83	0.86	0.89	0.91	0.93
24	0.54	0.70	0.80	0.86	0.90	0.93	0.95	0.97	0.98	0.99
36	0.62	0.79	0.87	0.92	0.95	0.97	0.98	0.99	0.99	1.00
48	0.69	0.85	0.92	0.95	0.97	0.98	0.99	1.00	1.00	1.00
60	0.74	0.88	0.94	0.97	0.98	0.99	1.00	1.00	1.00	1.00
72	0.78	0.91	0.96	0.98	0.99	1.00	1.00	1.00	1.00	1.00
84	0.81	0.93	0.97	0.99	0.99	1.00	1.00	1.00	1.00	1.00
96	0.84	0.94	0.98	0.99	1.00	1.00	1.00	1.00	1.00	1.00
108	0.86	0.96	0.98	0.99	1.00	1.00	1.00	1.00	1.00	1.00
120	0.88	0.96	0.99	0.99	1.00	1.00	1.00	1.00	1.00	1.00

Table 5.3: Ratio of Volatilities of Filtered and Original Signals: Monthly Data

When the filtered signal is used instead, we prove in the appendix that the variance of the bet becomes

$$Var(Bet^f) = Var\left(x_t - \frac{1}{m}\sum_{i=1}^{m} x_{t-i}\right) \qquad (5.27)$$

$$= \phi^2 \sigma_x^2$$

where

$$\phi^2 = \left\{1 - \left(\frac{2km-1}{m^2}\right)\left(\frac{1-k^m}{1-k}\right) + \frac{1+k}{m^2}\left[\left(\frac{m-1}{1-k}\right) - \frac{k\left(1-k^{m-1}\right)}{(1-k)^2}\right]\right\} \qquad (5.28)$$

Thus, the factor ϕ indicates the relative aggressiveness of the two strategies. $\phi > 1$ suggests that the filtered signal is more volatile than the original signal, while $\phi < 1$ suggests that the filtered signal is less volatile than the original signal. Without showing all the algebra and details, we prove that $0 \leq \phi \leq 1$ for all values of k and m. In Table 5.3 and Table 5.4, we compute the values of ϕ for different values of k and m, both for monthly and daily data.

Consistent with intuition, a filtered signal is less volatile than the original signal, whether we use monthly or daily data. Thus, a tactical bet based on a filtered signal is also less volatile. With monthly data, the volatility of the filtered signal is significantly lower only when mean reversion is slow (large k) and when a small moving average window size is used (small m). With daily data, the volatility of the filtered signal is almost identical to that of the original signal, unless the speed of mean reversion is extremely slow and a very small window size is used.

Accordingly, we can draw the conclusion that the volatility of bets of the strategies based on the original signal and the filtered signal are similar. Therefore, signal filtering has insignificant effects on the degree of aggressiveness of the strategy.

m	Speed of Mean Reversion Parameter: k									
Days	0.98	0.96	0.94	0.92	0.90	0.88	0.86	0.84	0.82	0.80
50	0.70	0.85	0.92	0.96	0.97	0.99	0.99	1.00	1.00	1.00
100	0.85	0.95	0.98	0.99	1.00	1.00	1.00	1.00	1.00	1.00
150	0.91	0.98	0.99	1.00	1.00	1.00	1.00	1.00	1.00	1.00
200	0.95	0.99	1.00	1.00	1.00	1.00	1.00	1.00	1.00	1.00
250	0.96	0.99	1.00	1.00	1.00	1.00	1.00	1.00	1.00	1.00
300	0.97	0.99	1.00	1.00	1.00	1.00	1.00	1.00	1.00	1.00
350	0.98	1.00	1.00	1.00	1.00	1.00	1.00	1.00	1.00	1.00
400	0.99	1.00	1.00	1.00	1.00	1.00	1.00	1.00	1.00	1.00
450	0.99	1.00	1.00	1.00	1.00	1.00	1.00	1.00	1.00	1.00
500	0.99	1.00	1.00	1.00	1.00	1.00	1.00	1.00	1.00	1.00

Table 5.4: Ratio of Volatilities of Filtered and Original Signals: Daily Data

5.7 Comparisons of Theoretical and Simulated Performance

We use simulation to further investigate the performance of tactical asset allocation strategies based on filtered signals and forward-looking equilibrium assumptions. Results from simulations are compared to the theoretical results established in previous sections. Following the previous chapters, we assume that the future risk premium, y_{t+1}, can be predicted by the current signal, x_t, according to the linear relationship:

$$y_{t+1} = a + bx_t + \varepsilon_{t+1} \tag{5.29}$$

where the signal is assumed to be mean-reverting following equation (5.17). By construction:

$$b = \rho \frac{\sigma_y}{\sigma_x} \tag{5.30}$$

Again, we assume that the bias is exogenous. This assumption can be relaxed if the effect of equilibrium assumptions on the value of the signal is well specified.

For example, if x is the expected risk premium, then the strategy is unbiased only when $a = 0$ and $b = 1$. Since a bias in the equilibrium value of the signal is equivalent to a bias in the equilibrium risk premium except for a difference in scale, it is technically easier to assume that there is a systematic bias in the expected risk premium, which is again denoted by δ. A positive δ indicates that the expected risk premium is systematically overestimated so that the strategy overweights stock, on the average. A negative δ indicates that the expected risk premium is systematically underestimated so that the strategy underweights stock, on the average.

According to the results of Chapter 4, the tactical bets of the unbiased and biased strategies are, respectively:

$$Bet_t = F\left[x_t - \mu_x\right] \tag{5.31}$$

and

$$Bet_t^b = F\left[(x_t - \mu_x) + \left(\frac{\delta}{b}\right)\right] \tag{5.32}$$

The tactical bet of the signal-filtering strategy can be obtained by simple substitution, with the results as follows:

$$Bet_t^f = F\left[(E\left(y_{t+1}\right) + \delta) - \frac{1}{m}\sum_{i=1}^{m}(E\left(y_{t+1-i}\right) + \delta)\right] \tag{5.33}$$

or

$$Bet_t^f = \frac{F}{b}\left[(a + bx_t + \delta) - \frac{1}{m}\sum_{i=1}^{m}(a + bx_{t-i} + \delta)\right] \tag{5.34}$$

For the biased and unbiased strategies, the analytical expressions for average and volatility of tactical bet, alpha, tracking error, and information ratio were derived in Chapter 4, and are restated below for ease of reference.

Average tactical bet:

$$\begin{aligned}
E[Bet_t] &= F\left(\frac{\delta}{b}\right) \\
&= F\left(\frac{\sigma_x}{\rho\sigma_y}\delta\right)
\end{aligned} \tag{5.35}$$

Variance of tactical bet:

$$Var[Bet_t] = F^2\sigma_x^2 \tag{5.36}$$

Total alpha:

$$\begin{aligned}
E[\alpha] &= F\left[\rho\sigma_x\sigma_y + \mu_y\left(\frac{\delta}{b}\right)\right] \\
&= F\left[\rho\sigma_x\sigma_y + \frac{\mu_y\sigma_x}{\rho\sigma_y}\delta\right]
\end{aligned} \tag{5.37}$$

Alpha of volatility capture:

$$\alpha_{vc} = F\left[\rho\sigma_x\sigma_y\right] \tag{5.38}$$

Alpha of bias:

$$\alpha_{bias} = F\left[\frac{\mu_y\sigma_x}{\rho\sigma_y}\delta\right] \tag{5.39}$$

Tracking error:

$$TE = F\sigma_x\sqrt{[\mu_y^2 + (1 + \rho^2)\sigma_y^2] + \left[\frac{1}{\rho^2}\delta^2 + 2\mu_y\delta\right]} \tag{5.40}$$

We use simulations to obtain comparative performance measures for the signal-filtering strategy. Although we can completely characterize the performance measures of the biased and unbiased strategies using the analytical expressions above, to ensure robustness we also report the simulated results of strategies with different degrees of bias. The specifications are intended to approximate reasonable monthly data:

- Number of observations simulated in each run: 25,000.

- Number of simulation runs: 100.

- Equilibrium value of risk premium, μ_y: 0.35 %.

- Standard deviation of risk premium, σ_y: 4.0 %.

- Equilibrium value of signal, μ_x: 0.0 %.

- Standard deviation of signal, σ_x: 2.0 %.

- Information coefficient = correlation of x_t and y_{t+1}, ρ: 0.2.

- Aggressiveness factor, F: 40.

- Speed of mean reversion parameter, k: 0.85, 0.90, 0.95.

- Moving average window size, m (months): 36, 72, 108, 144.

- Bias in expected risk premium expressed as a multiple of μ_y: +1.0, +0.5, -0.5, -1.0.

We use moving average window sizes of 36, 72, 108, and 144 months.. Four different degrees of bias in expected risk premium are studied, including overestimating ($\delta > 0$) and underestimating ($\delta < 0$) risk premium with $-\mu_y \leq \delta \leq +\mu_y$. We arbitrarily choose an aggressiveness factor of 40, which guarantees that the tactical bets are all small enough so that no short-selling of either asset is required. With the assumed mild degree of aggressiveness and a small positive bias of $0 \leq \delta \leq +\mu_y$, it has been shown in earlier chapters that the positively biased strategies will deliver higher information ratios than the unbiased strategy. Therefore, when the positive bias is filtered away by the moving average, the signal-filtering strategies will always deliver lower information ratios than the biased strategies. As a result, these cases are not very interesting to discuss. We put more focus on negatively biased strategies for the reason that the bias will hurt performance.

Since each simulation run corresponds to one sample, we repeat the whole process 100 times. The results reported in Table 5.5 are averages of all 100 simulation runs.[1] The amount of bias does not affect the performance of signal-filtering strategies, as all bias will be filtered away. As a result, we filter the expected risk premium of the strategy with a bias of $+\mu_y$.

---

[1] The headings of the columns stand for the alpha, tracking error, annualized information ratio, hit ratio, average bet, and standard deviation of bet, respectively.

		Alpha	T.E.	I.R.	H.R.	Avg. Bet	S. D. of Bet
k=0.85	Unbiased	0.77%	1.13%	0.68	56.4%	0	8%
	Bias $= +\mu_y$	0.87%	1.21%	0.72	56.8%	2.9%	8%
	Bias $= +0.5\mu_y$	0.82%	1.15%	0.71	56.7%	1.4%	8%
	Bias $= -0.5\mu_y$	0.71%	1.15%	0.62	55.8%	-1.6%	8%
	Bias $= -\mu_y$	0.66%	1.21%	0.55	55.0%	-3.1%	8%
	Filter: m = 36	0.65%	1.11%	0.58	55.5%	0	7.9%
	Filter: m = 72	0.71%	1.13%	0.63	55.9%	0	8%
	Filter: m = 108	0.73%	1.13%	0.64	56.0%	0	8%
	Filter: m = 144	0.74%	1.13%	0.65	56.1%	0	8%
k=0.90	Unbiased	0.77%	1.13%	0.68	56.4%	0	8%
	Bias $= +\mu_y$	0.87%	1.21%	0.72	56.8%	2.9%	8%
	Bias $= +0.5\mu_y$	0.82%	1.15%	0.71	56.7%	1.4%	8%
	Bias $= -0.5\mu_y$	0.71%	1.15%	0.62	55.8%	-1.6%	8%
	Bias $= -\mu_y$	0.66%	1.21%	0.55	55.0%	-3.1%	8%
	Filter: m = 36	0.58%	1.07%	0.54	55.1%	0	7.6%
	Filter: m = 72	0.67%	1.12%	0.62	55.6%	0	7.9%
	Filter: m = 108	0.70%	1.13%	0.62	55.9%	0	8%
	Filter: m = 144	0.72%	1.13%	0.64	56.0%	0	8%
k=0.95	Unbiased	0.77%	1.13%	0.68	56.4%	0	8%
	Bias $= +\mu_y$	0.87%	1.21%	0.72	56.8%	2.9%	8%
	Bias $= +0.5\mu_y$	0.82%	1.15%	0.71	56.7%	1.4%	8%
	Bias $= -0.5\mu_y$	0.71%	1.15%	0.62	55.8%	-1.6%	8%
	Bias $= -\mu_y$	0.66%	1.21%	0.55	55.0%	-3.1%	8%
	Filter: m = 36	0.43%	0.94%	0.45	54.2%	0	6.7%
	Filter: m = 72	0.57%	1.06%	0.54	55.0%	0	7.5%
	Filter: m = 108	0.63%	1.09%	0.58	55.4%	0	7.8%
	Filter: m = 144	0.67%	1.11%	0.60	55.6%	0	7.9%

Table 5.5: Simulated Trading Results

For ease of comparison, we plot the resulting information ratios of the signal-filtering strategies with different speeds of mean reversion parameter and moving average window size in Figure 5.3.

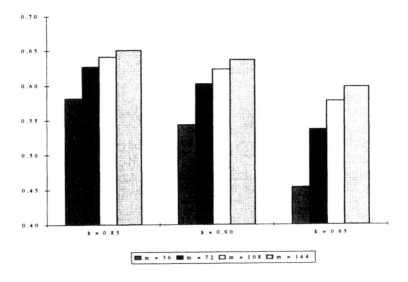

Figure 5.3: Information Ratios of Signal-Filtering Strategies

There are many interesting results, consistent with the analytical solutions documented thus far. Unless otherwise noted, we use the annualized information ratio as the measure of performance for comparison purposes. The important results are as follows.

1. Due to the incomplete retention of information, signal-filtering strategies always underperform the unbiased strategy. In the case of $k = 0.85$, for example, information ratios of the signal-filtering strategies range from 0.58 to 0.65 with increasing moving average window size, compared to the information ratio of the unbiased strategy of 0.68. In the case of $k = 0.95$, information ratios of the signal-filtering strategies range from 0.45 to 0.60.

2. Alpha, tracking error, information ratio, hit ratio, and standard deviation of bets of the signal-filtering strategy increase with the length of the moving average window. For example, for $k = 0.95$ and $m = 36$, the signal-filtering strategy delivers an alpha of 0.43%, tracking error of 0.94%, information ratio of 0.45, and hit ratio of 54.2%, with standard deviation of bet at 6.7%. For $k = 0.95$ and $m = 144$, the signal-filtering strategy delivers an alpha of 0.67%, tracking error of 1.11%, information ratio of 0.60, and hit ratio of 55.6%, with standard deviation of bet at 7.9%.

3. Alpha, tracking error, information ratio, hit ratio, and standard deviation of tactical bets of the signal-filtering strategy increase with the speed of mean reversion of the signal; that is, they all decrease with k. For example, for $k = 0.85$ and $m = 36$, the signal-filtering strategy delivers an alpha of 0.65%, tracking error of 1.11%, information ratio of 0.58, and hit ratio of 55.5%, with standard deviation of bet at 7.9%. For $k = 0.95$ and $m = 36$, the signal-filtering strategy delivers an alpha of only 0.43%, tracking error of 0.94%, information ratio of 0.45, and hit ratio of 54.2%, with standard deviation of bet at 6.7%.

4. With moderate moving average window length and speed of mean reversion of the signal, signal-filtering strategies outperform biased strategies that systematically underestimate the risk premium ($\delta < 0$). For example, at $k = 0.85$, the signal-filtering strategy with $m = 36$ delivers an information ratio of 0.58, outperforming the negatively biased strategy with $\delta = -\mu_y$, which has an information ratio of 0.55. For the moderately negatively biased strategy with $\delta = -0.5\mu_y$, which has an information ratio of 0.62, it is outperformed by the signal-filtering strategy with $m = 72$, which delivers an information ratio of 0.63.

5. Overestimating the risk premium ($\delta > 0$) leads to a positive average bet and higher alpha, tracking error, information ratio, and hit ratio than the unbiased strategy. These results are straightforward, and have been discussed previously.

6. Conversely, underestimating the risk premium ($\delta < 0$) leads to a negative average bet and lower alpha, tracking error, information ratio, and hit ratio than the unbiased strategy.

7. Any bias, whether it is positive or negative, leads to higher tracking error than the unbiased strategy, but the standard deviation of bets is unaffected. This is consistent with the result in Chapter 4, although with a very different time series approach.

For a meaningful comparison of the signal-filtering strategy and the forward-looking equilibrium assumption, it is important to understand what to expect from each strategy. Each strategy can outperform the other under different situations. Obviously, in the case of a positive bias that leads to average over-weighting of stock, the bias is in the investor's favor. Filtering with moving averages will only produce worse performance in this case. If the manager insists that a fair tactical asset allocation strategy should not overweight any one asset class on the average, however, then filtering seems to be a reasonable choice, unless the manager can assure that the strategy is unbiased.

In the case of a negative bias that leads to average underweighting of stock, the bias works against the manager. Whether to filter the signal or not comes down to a trade-off between a poorer information coefficient and removing the negative bias. As stated previously:

$$\text{Total Alpha} = \text{Alpha of Volatility Capture} + \text{Alpha of Bias} \qquad (5.41)$$

If the information coefficient is high enough so that the volatility capture component is large and positive, a negative bias does not necessarily lead to negative total alpha. As shown in Chapter 4, total alpha will be negative only when the negative bias is less than $-\left(\frac{\rho\sigma_y}{\mu_y}\right)^2 \mu_y$. In fact, in all our simulations, all negatively biased strategies still manage to have positive alphas.

In this case, we have to consider whether removing the negative alpha due to the negative bias is worthwhile, given that there is a deadweight cost of doing so in the form of a lower information coefficient, which, in turn, leads to a lower alpha of volatility capture. As shown analytically and empirically by the simulations, there is no general rule of thumb for this decision. Instead, the decision must be made depending on the particular situation, and of course, one's confidence in the forward-looking equilibrium assumptions.

In practice, all managers are biased. Furthermore, backtest results are not guaranteed to be accurate indicators of future performance, although they are good starting points of reference. Consequently, some degree of judgment is necessary to decide whether or not to filter the signals and how the signal should be filtered.

5.8   Concluding Remarks

There are several degrees of freedom that determine which strategy will outperform in the future, signal filtering versus forward-looking assumptions. In theory and with simulations, we demonstrate that under reasonable scenarios of the speed of mean reversion of the signal, extent of moving average window, and true equilibrium risk premium and volatility, a relatively high degree of accuracy of the forward-looking equilibrium assumption and a high quality of information are required to outperform the signal-filtering strategy. The final decision as to which strategy to use largely depends on one's confidence in the equilibrium assumptions.

Note also that the analysis in this chapter assumes that the true equilibrium is constant. The results thus suggest that the wider the moving average window, the better. A constant equilibrium is indeed an unfavorable condition for the signal-filtering strategy. When the true equilibrium is constantly changing, it is fair to expect the signal-filtering strategy to perform even better. In this case, further analysis is needed to choose the moving average window length, and we cannot make a fair comparison with the forward-looking assumption strategy unless the process of specifying the forward-looking assumptions is well defined. Nevertheless, we quantify the degree of accuracy required to make the forward-looking assumptions competitive with the signal-filtering strategy, and we illustrate that it is the changes in signals in the signal-filtering strategy, rather than the distance of the signal from the assumed equilibrium, that trigger a tactical trade.

Finally, our results also suggest that when equilibrium has to be specified, a moving average is a good starting point.

5.9 Appendix

This appendix outlines the proof of equations (5.22), (5.23), (5.27), and (5.28). All detailed matrix algebra is excluded.

By definition,

$$Cov\left(x_t - \frac{1}{m}\sum_{i=1}^{m} x_{t-i}, y_{t+1}\right) \tag{5.42}$$

$$= Cov\left(x_t, y_{t+1}\right) - \frac{1}{m}\sum_{i=1}^{m} Cov\left(x_{t-i}, y_{t+1}\right)$$

$$= \rho\sigma_x\sigma_y - \frac{1}{m}\sum_{i=1}^{m} k^i \rho\sigma_x\sigma_y$$

$$= \rho\sigma_x\sigma_y\left(1 - \frac{k}{m} \times \frac{1 - k^m}{1 - k}\right)$$

Given the assumed mean-reverting process of equation (5.17) for the signal x_t, one can easily show that $Cov\left(x_t, x_{t-i}\right) = k^i\sigma_x^2$. As a result,

$$Var\left(x_t - \frac{1}{m}\sum_{i=1}^{m} x_{t-i}\right) \tag{5.43}$$

$$= \begin{bmatrix} 1 & -\frac{1}{m} & -\frac{1}{m} & \cdots & -\frac{1}{m} \end{bmatrix} \begin{bmatrix} 1 & k & k^2 & \cdots & k^m \\ k & 1 & k & & k^{m-1} \\ k^2 & k & 1 & & k^{m-2} \\ \cdot & \cdot & \cdot & \cdots & \cdot \\ k^m & k^{m-1} & k^{m-2} & \cdots & 1 \end{bmatrix} \begin{bmatrix} 1 \\ -\frac{1}{m} \\ -\frac{1}{m} \\ \cdots \\ -\frac{1}{m} \end{bmatrix} \sigma_x^2$$

Expanding the quadratic form above and rearranging terms, we get

$$Var\left(x_t - \frac{1}{m}\sum_{i=1}^{m} x_{t-i}\right) \tag{5.44}$$

$$= \left[1 - \frac{(2km - 1) \times (1 - k^m)}{m^2(1 - k)} + \frac{1 + k}{m^2}\left(\frac{m - 1}{1 - k}\right) - \frac{k\left(1 - k^{m-1}\right)}{(1 - k)^2}\right]\sigma_x^2$$

which proves equations (5.27) and (5.28). Taking the ratio of covariance to the product of standard deviations thus establishes equations (5.22) and (5.23).

Chapter 6

Portfolio Construction I: Optimal Aggressiveness Factors

6.1 Introduction

In the previous chapters, we focus on bivariate asset allocation between stocks and bonds for the purpose of illustration. We also maintain the assumption that the manager uses only one signal, x_t, to predict the future risk premium, y_{t+1}, in making tactical bets. Or at the very least, the manager's information set can be represented by or reduced to a single variable. In reality, a tactical asset allocation portfolio will likely require many pairwise bets. In a simple portfolio of stocks, bonds, and cash, there are altogether three pairwise bets, namely, stock-bond, stock-cash, and bond-cash bets. In a global portfolio, the total number of pairwise bets can be even greater. In general, for every n different asset classes in the portfolio, there are $\frac{n(n-1)}{2}$ different pairwise bets. For example, in a global portfolio with investment in stocks and bonds of seven countries, there are altogether 91 different pairwise tactical bets to be made. It is therefore important to understand how to optimally combine these bets to form the final tactical portfolio.

Or, one can think of the problem from a different perspective. Imagine that there is only one pairwise bet to be made, say, between stocks and bonds. But this time, the manager uses several different signals. As long as the signals are less than perfectly correlated, they will have different characteristics and information content on future risk premiums. Consequently, each signal will lead to different tactical bets and, therefore, different performance characteristics such as information ratios and the like.[1]

---

[1] We ignore the case in which the signals are perfectly correlated but are different only in levels. In this case, performance will be different, but these are not very interesting cases to

No matter how many signals the manager uses, the final tactical bet can be thought of as a combination of all the bets made in accordance with each individual signal. It can also be interpreted as a tactical bet based on the composite signal. In this case, all signals are combined into a single composite signal before the tactical bet is made.

In practice, there are many different ways to combine several signals into a composite signal. Some may use principal components or factor analysis, while others may simply use the fitted value of a multiple regression of the risk premium on the set of different signals. Some may prefer prespecifying a set of different weights assigned to different signals in constructing the composite signals. These weights are very often argued as the Bayesian priors of the managers. Of course, other ad hoc procedures are used as well. In the more complicated cases, weights are allowed to change over time, or as functions of other variables so that the resulting model can be highly non-linear.

The purpose of this chapter is to analyze how different bets should be combined to form the final tactical portfolio. Generally speaking, the focus is on the optimal combination of information, whether it is information on different pairs of assets or different information on the same pair of assets.

As always, it is necessary to define what we mean by optimal combination. Unless it is otherwise stated, the objective is always to maximize the overall information ratio of the tactical portfolio, as this is more consistent with the way asset allocation managers are evaluated. Based on the objective function, the concepts behind the "Alpha Tracking Error Efficient Frontier" are articulated. We demonstrate that such a framework has the potential to significantly increase the information ratio.

Five case studies are discussed to illustrate potential applications of the framework developed in this chapter. When forward-looking inputs are added, this framework can be applied to set trading ranges for all assets in the asset allocation portfolio, as well as to pick the optimal mix of asset allocation strategies or managers. It also provides insights on the reasonable number of pairwise bets, or the number of signals to be used for the same pairwise bet so that most of the information is captured.

This has important implications in practice. For example, it is not rare that asset allocation managers will use some two dozen signals for making a stock-bond bet. While managers may argue that such an approach takes advantage of a wide range of information, our results suggest that to a large extent most of these signals are likely to be redundant. Too many signals will only reduce the transparency of the model and increase the work load of the manager and the trading system, while adding only insignificant marginal value.

Finally, we use the same framework to analyze the cases for and against making a structural bet for the higher-return asset. Consistent with the results in Chapter 4, we conclude that a negative structural bet always diminishes the overall information ratio, while a wide range of positive structural bets can increase the overall information ratio.

---

discuss.

To derive the theoretical results, we use the case of multiple pairwise bets as an example. It should be clear that the framework developed in this chapter can also be applied to the case of multiple signals for the same pairwise bet. As a practical example, we also use the low-frequency (LF) signal and the high-frequency (HF) signal (first discussed in Chapter 3 for the stock-bond tactical decision) to illustrate an optimal combination of bets in one case study.

6.2 Multiple Pairwise Bets

When there is more than one pairwise bet in an asset allocation portfolio, setting the appropriate aggressiveness factor for each bet is critically important. The set of aggressiveness factors produces not only different trading ranges for the asset classes, but also very different investment performance. This is particularly true when the correlations of alphas of different pairwise bets are low. A typical example is in a global asset allocation portfolio, where bets such as between German stock and Canadian bonds, or between French bonds and US cash, are common.

While portfolio theory gives optimal portfolio weights of each risky security in a portfolio based on mean-variance optimization, similar theory for asset allocation is not yet well articulated. For instance, in a simple three-way asset allocation among stocks, bonds, and cash in a strategic benchmark portfolio of, say, 60/30/10, how should the ranges of weights of each asset class be determined? An obvious criterion is the binding condition that the sum of weights should be equal to 100%. While imposing this condition is straightforward, setting the optimal ranges arbitrarily will ignore the tremendous potential benefits of diversification among different pairwise allocation bets within the same overall portfolio.

In the asset allocation industry, a standard criterion to evaluate a manager is based on the information ratio. A high information ratio indicates that the manager is able to add a higher alpha for the same amount of tracking error. This chapter develops a simple framework for optimal combination of information so as to maximize the overall information ratio. Following previous chapters, we introduce the term "aggressiveness factor" in asset allocation, which plays a role similar to that of portfolio weights in standard portfolio optimization.

6.2.1 Formulation of Problem

To determine the optimal deviations from the benchmark portfolio weights, the asset allocation manager must form a view on the relative attractiveness of each asset class. The most conventional approach is based on expected returns. The view may be expressed as a raw signal based on the difference of expected returns, or on the difference of expected returns minus the equilibrium value, which is more consistent with the definition of a neutral stance in the asset allocation industry. For example, for the pairwise bet between stocks and bonds, the view is expressed as

$$Signal_t = (E[R_{S,t+1}] - E[R_{B,t+1}]) - (\overline{R}_S - \overline{R}_B) \qquad (6.1)$$

where $E[R_{S,t+1}]$ and $E[R_{B,t+1}]$ are the expected returns of stocks and bonds from time t to time $t+1$ based on the information set available at time t, and $\overline{R}_S$ and $\overline{R}_B$ are the equilibrium returns of stocks and bonds, respectively. In this way, the asset allocation manager overweights stock when the signal is positive, and underweights stock when the signal is negative. This trading rule has been discussed in Chapter 2 and Chapter 4.

While the direction and the magnitude of the tactical bets or deviations from the benchmark portfolio are determined according to the signal, the magnitude of the bets also depends on other factors. For instance, the manager may be more confident in the signal between stocks and bonds than the signal between stocks and cash, so that the manager is more aggressive in making the stock-bond bet. In addition, since the manager is evaluated according to the overall information ratio, there are potential diversification benefits among different pairwise bets to minimize the total tracking error of the asset allocation portfolio at the same level of targeted alpha. In achieving this, the relative aggressiveness in making different bets needs to be set appropriately.

6.2.2　Definitions

The manager is assumed to have n pairwise tactical bets to make. To simplify, we also assume that the manager has already combined information such that each pairwise bet is made depending on a composite signal. For ease of reference, we list the definitions of all variables to be used in deriving the theory. Time subscripts are dropped as these should be understood.

- N: Number of pairwise bets.

- **x**: An $N \times 1$ vector of composite signals.

- **F**: An $N \times 1$ vector of aggressiveness factors.

- $\overline{\alpha}$: An $N \times 1$ vector of alphas for the N pairwise bets when all aggressiveness factors are set to 1.0, that is, the alphas from trading the raw signals.

- **Q**: An $N \times N$ covariance matrix of alphas from trading the raw signals; that is, the covariance matrix of the elements in $\overline{\alpha}$.

- λ: Lagrangian multiplier

- **Bet**: An $N \times 1$ vector of tactical bets.

Generally, the size of the tactical bet between each pair of assets is determined as a multiple of the signal. That is:

$$Bet_i = F_i x_i \qquad (6.2)$$

for $i = 1, 2, ..., N$. The linear investment rule and aggressiveness factor are discussed in detail in Chapter 2 and Chapter 4. The first task is to determine the optimal vector of aggressiveness factors, $\mathbf{F}$, and the optimal trading ranges for each asset can then be set accordingly with the range of each signal. When the alphas of each pairwise bet are less than perfectly correlated, there is an optimal vector of aggressiveness factors so that diversification of tracking errors is obtained at each targeted alpha, and thus the maximum possible information ratio given the quality of information can be attained.

Conceptually, this is similar to mean-variance optimization in portfolio construction in setting the optimal portfolio weights of each asset. There are at least two important differences:

1. The sum of portfolio weights in a traditional efficient portfolio problem is equal to one; in asset allocation, such an equality constraint is irrelevant, as the aggressiveness factors can assume any positive value, and thus, sum to any value as well.

2. Inputs to a traditional optimization problem, including the expected returns and covariance matrix, are fixed, whatever the resulting optimal portfolio weights. In asset allocation, alphas, tracking errors, and covariance of alphas all change with aggressiveness factors.

To tackle the problem, it is necessary to realize that both pairwise alphas and elements of the covariance matrix of alphas are linearly proportional to the aggressiveness factors when no constraint is binding. For example, consider two pairwise allocation strategies, i and j, which may denote stock-bond and stock-cash allocation strategies, respectively. The alphas, tracking errors, and the covariance of the alphas are stated without proof as

$$\alpha_i = F_i \overline{\alpha}_i \tag{6.3}$$

$$TE_i = F_i \bullet \overline{TE}_i \tag{6.4}$$

and

$$Cov(\alpha_i, \alpha_j) = F_i F_j Cov(\overline{\alpha}_i, \overline{\alpha}_j) \tag{6.5}$$

where $\overline{\alpha}$ and $\overline{TE}$ denote the performance measures of the pairwise bet when the aggressiveness factor is set to 1; that is, when the raw signals are traded. Equation (6.5) indicates that the covariance of alphas of two different pairwise bets with aggressiveness factors F_i and F_j, respectively, is simply equal to the product of the aggressiveness factors and the covariance of the alphas of the two bets with unit aggressiveness factors. Thus, we can work with the pairwise alphas and their corresponding covariance matrix with all aggressiveness factors being equal to 1, as if they were some individual securities in a portfolio with fixed expected returns, variances, and covariances. In this way, aggressiveness factors in asset allocation decisions play a role similar to that of portfolio weights in portfolio construction.

6.3   Optimal Aggressiveness Factors

To formally derive the optimal aggressiveness factors (OAF) framework, we state the problem as

$$\min_{\mathbf{F}} \frac{1}{2}\mathbf{F}'\mathbf{QF} \tag{6.6}$$

subject to

$$\mathbf{F}'\overline{\alpha} = \alpha \tag{6.7}$$

where $F_i \geq 0, i = 1, 2, ..., N$.

For each level of target total alpha for the whole asset allocation portfolio, α, we minimize half of the variance of α. We constrain all aggressiveness factors to be non-negative. Provided that the non-negative constraints on F_i are not binding, the optimal vector of aggressiveness factors, $\mathbf{F}^*$, can be solved analytically by the standard Kuhn-Tucker method.

We first form the Lagrangian

$$L = \frac{1}{2}\mathbf{F}'\mathbf{QF} + \lambda\left(\alpha - \mathbf{F}'\overline{\alpha}\right) \tag{6.8}$$

The first-order conditions are

$$\frac{\partial L}{\partial \mathbf{F}} = \mathbf{QF} - \lambda\overline{\alpha} \tag{6.9}$$

$\Rightarrow$

$$\mathbf{F}^* = \lambda \mathbf{Q}^{-1}\overline{\alpha} \tag{6.10}$$

Substituting into the target total alpha constraint in equation (6.7), we get

$$\overline{\alpha}'\lambda\mathbf{Q}^{-1}\overline{\alpha} = \alpha \tag{6.11}$$

$\Rightarrow$

$$\lambda = \frac{\alpha}{\overline{\alpha}'\mathbf{Q}^{-1}\overline{\alpha}} \tag{6.12}$$

Thus, the optimal vector of aggressiveness factors that minimizes variance of alpha for any target total alpha is given by

$$\mathbf{F}^* = \frac{\alpha}{\overline{\alpha}'\mathbf{Q}^{-1}\overline{\alpha}}\mathbf{Q}^{-1}\overline{\alpha} \tag{6.13}$$

The resulting minimum total tracking error of the tactical portfolio is given by

$$TE^* = \sqrt{\mathbf{F}^{*\prime}\mathbf{QF}^*} \tag{6.14}$$

which, after substituting equation (6.13) and rearranging, is shown to be

$$TE^* = \frac{\alpha}{\sqrt{\overline{\alpha}'\mathbf{Q}^{-1}\overline{\alpha}}} \tag{6.15}$$

Dividing the targeted alpha by the minimum tracking error of equation (6.15) gives the maximum information ratio achievable as

$$IR^* = \sqrt{\overline{\alpha}'\mathbf{Q}^{-1}\overline{\alpha}} \tag{6.16}$$

A plot of the target total alpha against the minimized tracking error of equation (6.15) is known as the *alpha tracking error (A-TE) efficient frontier*.

Some interesting features of the solutions above are worth discussing. First, consider any two optimal asset allocation portfolios at two different levels of target total alphas, α_1 and α_2, along the A-TE efficient frontier. Let $\mathbf{F}_1^*$ and $\mathbf{F}_2^*$ be the two optimal vectors of aggressiveness factors for the two levels of target total alphas, respectively. By definition, the covariance of the alphas of these two TAA portfolios is

$$Cov(\alpha_1, \alpha_2) = \mathbf{F}_1^{*'}\mathbf{Q}\mathbf{F}_2^* \tag{6.17}$$

Applying equation (6.13) and rearranging, we can show that

$$Cov(\alpha_1, \alpha_2) = \frac{\alpha_1\alpha_2}{\overline{\alpha}'\mathbf{Q}^{-1}\overline{\alpha}} \tag{6.18}$$

Dividing the covariance by the corresponding tracking errors according to equation (6.15) establishes the result that

$$Corr(\alpha_1, \alpha_2) = +1 \tag{6.19}$$

That is, any optimal tactical portfolios along the A-TE efficient frontier are perfectly positively correlated. This result seems more obvious when one recalls that all portfolios along the frontier are formed on the basis of the same set of information, and intuitively there is only one optimal way to use the same information set so as to attain the maximum information ratio, given the quality of information. The only difference between any two optimal portfolios along the frontier is by a ratio of their target total alphas. For the same maximum attainable information ratio, a higher level of target total alpha can be attained simply by increasing the levels of the whole vector of optimal aggressiveness factors for all pairwise bets.

Second, in contrast to the mean-variance portfolio frontier which is a parabola in a mean-variance space and a hyperbola in a mean-standard deviation space, the A-TE efficient frontier is a straight line in the alpha tracking error space. Equation (6.15) shows that the minimum tracking error is linearly proportional to the target total alpha, with the proportional factor being the inverse of the maximum attainable information ratio. The relationship is as depicted in Figure 6.1.

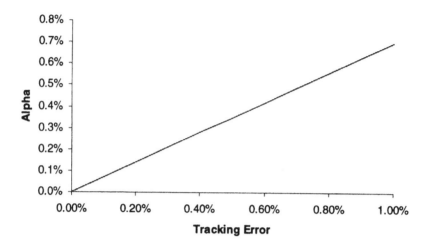

Figure 6.1: Alpha-Tracking Error Efficient Frontier

The relationship is a straight line because the elements of the vector of the optimal aggressiveness factor, $\mathbf{F^*}$, do not sum to one, which is incorporated into the mathematical results. To further understand this, recall that the typical portfolio frontier of any two securities with $-1 < correlation < +1$ is a curve, starting from one security with weights $(1, 0)$ and ending at another security with weights $(0, 1)$. On the contrary, in the A-TE efficient frontier of any two pairwise tactical bets, the minimum tracking error is obviously zero, with aggressiveness factors $(0, 0)$. That is, the minimum tracking error is attained by simply holding the benchmark portfolio and not making any tactical asset allocation decisions. As a result, the A-TE efficient frontier in Figure 6.1 starts at the origin.

Finally, our solutions are closely related to and largely consistent with those of active portfolio management by Grinold (1989, 1994) and Grinold and Kahn (1995). The Fundamental Law of Active Management of Grinold and Kahn states that, in an active portfolio of stocks, the information ratio of the portfolio is approximately equal to the product of the information coefficient of each bet and the square root of the total number of bets made in the portfolio. Grinold and Kahn (1995) also argue that information is approximately additive in square form. To arrive at their conclusions, one has to assume that the information ratios of all bets are the same, and their alphas are independent.

When the same set of assumptions is made in our problem, equation (6.16) can be rewritten as

$$IR^* \approx IR \times \sqrt{N} \tag{6.20}$$

where IR is the information ratio of all bets, assumed to be the same, and N is the total number of bets. Yet since asset allocation decisions deal with broad asset classes that are well diversified, their returns are largely driven by sets of common factors. It is therefore unlikely that alphas of the decisions or signals are independent. As a result, the Fundamental Law of Active Management is not applicable in asset allocation. Instead, the full expression of the optimal aggressiveness factor must be used.

6.4   Alternative Interpretations of Optimal Aggressiveness Factors

While the analytical solution procedure to derive the OAF is tractable, it may still be difficult to understand the economic meanings of the OAF as well as to see what it would lead us to hold in an asset allocation portfolio. With some additional matrix algebra, we can restate the OAF in a more compelling way. We apply some well-established results of matrix partition without proof. Since the Lagrange multiplier, λ, is a scalar, it is easier to use equation (6.10) instead of equation (6.13) for the time being. Generally speaking, λ depends on the target level of alpha, denoted as α, and the functional form of the utility function.

The inverse of the covariance matrix of alpha plays a critical role in determining the optimal aggressiveness of each pairwise bet. The same is true in a standard mean-variance optimization problem, in which the inverse of the covariance matrix of asset returns is an important determinant of optimal portfolio weights. Therefore, some results of Stevens (1998) are also valid in our OAF problem. Applying equation (8) of Stevens (1998), the inverse of the matrix $\mathbf{Q}$ can be rewritten as

$$\mathbf{Q}^{-1} = \begin{bmatrix} \dfrac{1}{Q_{11}\left(1-R_1^2\right)} & -\dfrac{\beta_{12}}{Q_{11}\left(1-R_1^2\right)} & \cdots & -\dfrac{\beta_{1N}}{Q_{11}\left(1-R_1^2\right)} \\ -\dfrac{\beta_{21}}{Q_{22}\left(1-R_2^2\right)} & \dfrac{1}{Q_{22}\left(1-R_2^2\right)} & \cdots & -\dfrac{\beta_{2N}}{Q_{22}\left(1-R_2^2\right)} \\ \vdots & \vdots & \ddots & \vdots \\ -\dfrac{\beta_{N1}}{Q_{NN}(1-R_n^2)} & -\dfrac{\beta_{N2}}{Q_{NN}\left(1-R_N^2\right)} & \cdots & \dfrac{1}{Q_{NN}\left(1-R_N^2\right)} \end{bmatrix} \quad (6.21)$$

where Q_{ij} is the ith-jth element of the covariance matrix of $\overline{\alpha}$; β_{ij} for $i \neq j$ is the coefficient on the alpha of the pairwise bet j in a multiple regression of the alpha of the pairwise bet i on alphas of all other $N-1$ pairwise bets; and R_i^2 is the squared multiple regression coefficient of the same regression. For example, Q_{11} is the variance of the alpha of the first pairwise bet, or the square of its tracking error. Q_{12} is the covariance of alphas of the first and second pairwise bets. In a multiple regression of alpha of the first pairwise bet on alphas of all other $N-1$ pairwise bets, β_{12} is the coefficient on the alpha of the second pairwise bet, and the resulting squared multiple regression coefficient is denoted as R_1^2.

Recall that the squared multiple regression coefficient measures the proportion of variance of the dependent variable explained by the set of independent variables. As a result, the denominator of each element in $\mathbf{Q}^{-1}$, $Q_{ii}\left(1 - R_i^2\right)$, measures the variance of the alpha of the pairwise bet i that cannot be explained by the alphas of all other $N - 1$ pairwise bets. Technically, it is equal to the variance of the error term in the multiple regression.

With $\mathbf{Q}^{-1}$ fully expressed as in equation (6.21), we can now draw more insights from the OAF results. Consider the simplest special case in which the alphas of all pairwise bets are independent. This is obviously an unrealistic case, but nevertheless, it is an interesting case for articulating the concepts. In the case of mutually independent alphas, all correlation coefficients and covariances of alphas are zero. Therefore, all off-diagonal elements of $\mathbf{Q}^{-1}$ are zero. In addition, all R_i^2 are zero as well.

Applying equation (6.10), it is straightforward to show that the optimal aggressiveness factor for pairwise bet i is proportional to the ratio of its alpha to the square of its tracking error. In other words, it is proportional to the information ratio, but inversely proportional to the tracking error.

In the general and realistic case with dependent alphas, the solution is considerably more complicated. Applying equation (6.10) again, the optimal aggressiveness factor for pairwise bet i is given by

$$F_i^* = \lambda \frac{\overline{\alpha}_i - \sum_{i \neq j} \beta_{ij} \overline{\alpha}_j}{Q_{ii}\left(1 - R_i^2\right)} \tag{6.22}$$

Equation (6.22) may look forbidding, but a closer look at its components should reveal that the key concepts behind optimization are embedded in it.

As we explained previously, the denominator is the variance of the alpha of bet i that cannot be explained by the alphas of all other bets. In a multiple regression, the coefficients are the least-squares estimates that minimize the residual variance. Therefore, the denominator is the non-diversifiable part of bet i's variance. Alternatively, we may interpret it as the idiosyncratic, specific, or unhedgeable active risk of making bet i in the whole asset allocation strategy.

In any simple regression, the regression line has to pass through the point of the means. Therefore, the part of the level of the dependent variable that cannot be accounted for by the levels of the independent variables is in the intercept term of the regression. Technically, the numerator of equation (6.22) is equal to the intercept term in the multiple regression of $\overline{\alpha}_i$ on the other $N - 1$ $\overline{\alpha}_j$, where $i \neq j$.

The expression of OAF with dependent alphas is conceptually the same, except that it uses the regression-adjusted form. It uses the parts of the alpha and the variance of the bet that cannot be accounted for by the other bets. That is, the OAF for a particular bet is proportional to its idiosyncratic information ratio, but inversely proportional to its idiosyncratic tracking error.

In short, in the OAF framework, it is the non-substitutable information content and contribution to the total asset allocation strategy of a particular bet that determines its weight in the strategy. The same interpretation and conclusion can be made in the case of a multiple signals problem for the same pairwise bet. The signal that has the highest non-substitutable information content is assigned the highest weight.

6.5 Case Studies

We apply the OAF framework to several different asset allocation problems.

6.5.1 Case 1: Stock-Bond-Cash Asset Allocation

To illustrate how the OAF framework can be used to achieve the highest possible information ratio, we consider a three-way asset allocation among stocks, bonds, and cash. Some forward-looking assumptions are required to implement the framework. The forward-looking assumptions for stock-bond (SB), stock-cash (SC), and bond-cash (BC) in the first example are

	Stock-Bond	Stock-Cash	Bond-Cash
Alpha	0.25%	0.10%	0.20%
Tracking Error	0.42%	0.29%	0.33%
Information Ratio	0.60	0.35	0.60

The correlation matrix of the alphas of these three pairwise bets is assumed to be

$$
\begin{bmatrix}
1.0 & 0.6 & 0.3 \\
0.6 & 1.0 & 0.05 \\
0.3 & 0.05 & 1.0
\end{bmatrix}
$$

Recall that the performance measures are based on trading the raw signals, or with all aggressiveness factors set to one. In practice, the performance assumptions will depend on the manager's own assessment, using either the historical track record or a model incorporating signals and expected returns on each asset class. For instance, if the managers use an econometric model to generate expected returns, the conditional expected values, variances, and covariances can easily be obtained, and used as forward-looking assumptions. The inputs and the analytical expressions produce the optimal aggressiveness factors shown in Figure 6.2.

The maximum attainable overall information ratio for the whole asset allocation portfolio, given the quality of information, is computed as 0.75, higher than the information ratio of any individual pairwise strategy. Obviously, the improvement in the overall information ratio is due to the diversification of overall tracking error when appropriate aggressiveness factors are assigned to each pairwise strategy. For example, at a target alpha of 1%, the optimal aggressiveness factors for SB, SC, and BC are 1.76, 0.50, and 2.54, respectively, with a minimum tracking error of 1.34%.

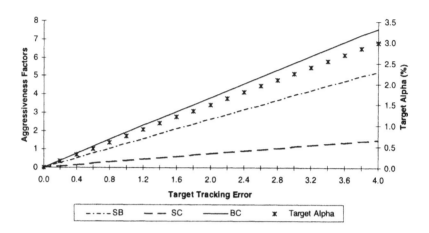

Figure 6.2: Optimal Aggressiveness Factors of Multiple Bets

As Figure 6.2 shows, BC is assigned the highest aggressiveness factor, followed by SB and SC. The reasoning is as follows. Although SB has a higher alpha than BC, both SB and BC have the same information ratio. This means that, for the same amount of tracking error, both strategies deliver the same amount of alpha. For example, we can assign an aggressiveness factor of 1.00 to SB, and an aggressiveness factor of 1.25 (= 0.25%/0.20%) to BC such that both strategies are expected to deliver the same amount of alpha (0.25%) with the same amount of tracking error (0.42%). In other words, SB and BC are not different from each other when judged individually.

The fact that the optimizer assigns a higher aggressiveness factor to BC than to SB becomes clear once we look at the correlation matrix of alphas as well. Notice that BC has the lowest correlations with the other two strategies, implying that, apart from delivering the highest information ratio, it also provides more diversification benefits to the overall asset allocation portfolio. As a result, it receives the highest aggressiveness factor from the optimizer. In the case of SB versus SC, although SC has lower correlations with the others than SB, it is still dominated by SB because of its substantially lower information ratio.

Once the optimal aggressiveness factors are determined, the optimal trading ranges of each asset class can also be set in accordance with the volatilities of the corresponding signals. For example, the trading range for stock will depend on the aggressiveness factors for the SB and SC bets, as well as the ranges of the signals for these bets. Obviously, these trading ranges may not be feasible for all benchmark portfolios. For a benchmark portfolio of, say, 60/35/5 in stocks, bonds, and cash, the benchmark constraint on cash can easily become binding so that the minimum position on cash is zero. Or, depending on the expected returns model of the asset allocation manager, the signals can be volatile enough so that the benchmark constraints are reached. In this way, either the lower bound or the upper bound of the trading range is constrained by the benchmark position in that asset class. The problem will have to be solved numerically.

6.5.2   Case 2: Optimal Mix of Managers

The same OAF framework can be applied by investment advisors, consultants, or asset allocation clients to pick the optimal mix of asset allocation managers, provided that the objective is to maximize the overall information ratio. With appropriate expected performance measures, historical track record, and correlations of performance among managers, the advisor will be able to determine the optimal relative mix of managers so that the maximum information ratio is delivered.

For instance, consider three asset allocation managers in the universe, denoted as i, j, and k. Given their expected performance characteristics, the optimal aggressiveness factors for three different managers are, say, determined as F_i, F_j, and F_k, respectively. The optimal proportions of funds to be managed by each manager are thus, respectively, $\frac{F_i}{F_i+F_j+F_k}$, $\frac{F_j}{F_i+F_j+F_k}$, and $\frac{F_k}{F_i+F_j+F_k}$.

6.5.3   Case 3: Multiple Signals

Next, we study a composite signal of the high-frequency signal and the low-frequency signal for the stock-bond tactical decision. The HF and LF signals are used as examples in Chapter 2 and Chapter 4. Using the OAF framework, we can illustrate how different combinations of the two signals into a composite signal can affect the information ratio of the strategy.

For ease of reference, the performance of the two signals from January 1987 to March 1999 was:

	LF	HF
Alpha	0.32%	0.80%
Tracking Error	1.00%	1.00%
Information Ratio	0.32	0.80

The correlation between the alphas of LF and HF is 0.52. With these as inputs to equation (6.13), the optimal combination of the two signals for a 1.00% target alpha is determined as $(-0.20, 1.33)$, giving the maximum attainable information ratio of 0.81.

This is an interesting example. When the LF and HF signals are applied individually, both deliver positive information ratios, although their alphas are correlated with a coefficient of 0.52. Therefore, both signals have positive information for the future risk premium. On the other hand, the optimal combination of the signals for maximizing the information ratio suggests that one should bet -0.20 unit of LF and 1.33 unit of HF.

A good analogy is ordinary least-squares linear regression. It is well understood that when the regression is misspecified, such as with missing variables, the least-squares coefficients are biased. The direction of bias depends on the full covariance matrix of the dependent variables and all independent variables. Therefore, the coefficients in a misspecified regression can have the wrong signs. The problem is particularly significant when the independent variables are highly correlated, the so-called near-multicollinearity problem. In this case, estimates of coefficients are very imprecise and thus produce large standard errors.

In this particular case study with signals LF and HF, correlation of alphas is 0.52. Although this is still far from a perfect correlation of 1, it suggests that the information content of the two signals is overlapped to some extent. Since the information ratio of the HF is much higher than that of the LF, it is entirely possible that one should bet against the LF signal so as to free up more room to bet on the HF signal, which in turn maximizes the overall information ratio.

Finally, we experiment with different combinations of LF and HF, by fixing the aggressiveness factor for HF at 1 and varying the aggressiveness factor for LF from -1 to 1. The resulting information ratios of these combinations are plotted in Figure 6.3.

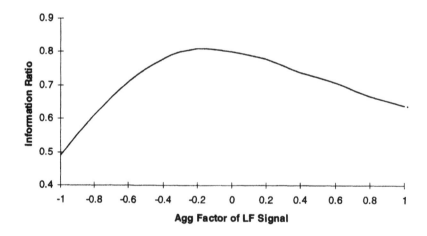

Figure 6.3: Information Ratios of Combinations of LF and HF Signals

As expected, the maximum information ratio of 0.81 is achieved at an aggressiveness factor of $\frac{-0.20}{1.33} = -0.15$ for the LF when the aggressiveness factor of HF is fixed at 1.0.

6.5.4 Case 4: How Many Signals? How Many Bets?

As we briefly noted earlier, some managers claim to be tracking dozens of signals for making the same bet. Interestingly, many managers treat a high number of signals as one of the strengths of their models. It cannot be denied that being able to track many different signals is valuable in some sense. This is not without costs, however. Tracking too many signals will require more investment professionals and thus higher overhead costs. A model with numerous signals will also overload system requirements and computing time, and be more difficult and time-consuming to explain to clients. More important, too many signals in a model also makes data mining a far greater risk.

In mean-variance portfolio analysis, it has been known for some time that one needs not hold the entire investment universe in order to achieve a decent degree of diversification. For reasonable correlations among different risky securities, several dozen securities should be enough to achieve most of the attainable diversification benefits embedded in the entire universe. The same insight applies to asset allocation as well. Of course, in reality, the results are highly dependent on the circumstances. Different managers will have different capabilities in extracting signals for different asset classes.

A generic example exemplifies the implications of the OAF framework. Assume that twelve less-than-perfectly correlated signals can completely characterize the time series properties of the risk premium between stocks and bonds. In other words, variables other than these twelve signals incorporate no unique information on the future risk premium, and are thus irrelevant. For ease of illustration, assume further that the correlation coefficients of the alphas of these signals are the same. We study three scenarios in which the correlations are 0, 0.25, and 0.5. All signals have the same performance statistics, with alpha of 0.3%, tracking error of 1.0%, and thus an information ratio of 0.3.

Applying equation (6.16), we can compute the maximum attainable information ratios, given the numbers of signals included in making the tactical bets. The result is plotted in Figure 6.4.

As revealed in the figure, the marginal improvement of the information ratio diminishes with each additional signal. Consider the example of 0.5 correlations among alphas. The maximum attainable information ratio when all signals are included according to the OAF is equal to 0.41. When the number of signals included increases from one to two, the information ratio is improved from 0.30 to 0.36. When eight signals are included, the information ratio is indistinguishable from the global maximum of 0.41 at two decimal places. In fact, if the manager is satisfied with achieving 90% of the maximum achievable information ratio, which is about 0.37, a mere three signals out of the universe of twelve all more than enough!

In the case of 0.25 correlation coefficients of alphas, six signals are enough to achieve an information ratio of 0.48, which is 90% of the maximum achievable information ratio of 0.53. The results are intuitive, as lower correlations imply that the information content of these signals is largely unique, and there is only a small degree of overlap. As a result, it will take more signals to capture the

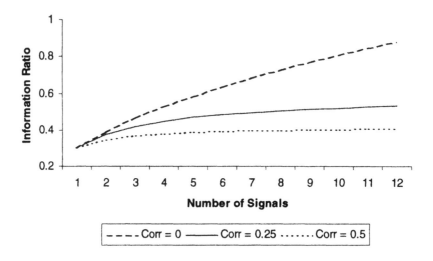

Figure 6.4: Maximum Information Ratio as a Function of Number of Signals or Bets

same degree of information than when correlations are higher. Finally, in the unrealistic case of zero correlations, information in each signal is completely unique, and the marginal contribution of each signal in the overall information ratio is almost additive.

These simple examples should make one seriously reconsider whether the marginal benefits of including a great number of signals are great enough to be worthwhile, given the various costs of doing so.

These results also shed light on the number of bets in a total tactical portfolio. In the investment industry, active asset allocation is generally accepted as a product with a relatively low information ratio, for the number of bets involved is relatively small compared to that of active stock selection in active equity products. As a result, only limited diversification opportunities are available. The example similarly shows that moving from a domestic tactical asset allocation portfolio of stocks, bonds, and cash with only three pairwise bets into a global portfolio that can easily have several dozen bets should greatly enhance opportunities of adding value and thus of achieving a higher information ratio. Nevertheless, it is likely that fewer than a dozen bets are necessary for attaining most of the maximum attainable information ratio when all pairwise bets are made.

We might also think about the effects of the EMU on a global tactical portfolio in the same way. European countries, excluding the United Kingdom, account for 13 of the 22 MSCI Developed Markets universe. If all 22 markets are being traded in the global portfolio, merging 13 European markets into one

EMU may not have a great impact on overall performance, unless the manager has unique information about these European countries, and correlations of alphas with other bets are low. On the other hand, if only those markets with liquid futures contracts are traded (which typically includes Australia, Canada, France, Germany, Italy, Japan, Spain, the United Kingdom, and the United States), EMU in effect reduces the number of countries in the portfolio from nine to six. If only stocks and bonds of these countries are traded, EMU reduces the number of pairwise bets from 36 to 15.

At first, this may appear to be a significant reduction in the number of decisions, but again, the exact effects on overall information ratio will depend on other parameters. As some of our examples have shown, the effects of the EMU on global tactical portfolios may have been overstated.

6.5.5   Case 5: Structural Bets?

In the investment industry, whether or not one should make a structural bet on assets with higher returns is one of the most controversial issues. For example, in asset allocation, what does a constant overweight of stocks against bonds do to the overall portfolio? Since the equity risk premium is believed to be positive, overweighting stock over a long enough horizon will add value, so this simple structural bet may be viewed as a potential source of alpha. In style rotation, should value be overweighted against growth on average in order to capture the value premium documented by Fama and French (1998), among others?[2] In size portfolios, should small be overweighted against large on average so as to capture the size premium first documented in Banz (1981), and more recently in Siegel (1998)?[3]

In Chapter 4, we show in a dynamic time series setting that while a negative structural bet will always diminish the information ratio, a positive structural bet will increase the information ratio only up to the limit when it is not so dominating that it is competing tracking error away from other informative signals.

In our last case study, we analyze the effect of a structural bet on the overall information ratio based on the OAF framework. As our theoretical derivation has shown, the covariance matrix of alphas plays a critical role in determining the optimal combination of information and, subsequently, the information ratio. We therefore need to come up with some decent assumptions of the covariance matrix of alphas of signals and alpha of a structural bet, as well as some other performance statistics of the structural bet.

To begin, we once again use the stock-bond pairwise decision as our example. We first look at the historical stock-bond risk premium of the United

---

[2] Note that the existence of a value premium is not settled. For instance, the average returns of the BARRA/S&P Growth and Value indexes from 1978 to early 1999 are moving toward each other, so that the average premium in the last two decades is close to zero.

[3] While the long-term historical return of a small-stock portfolio is higher than that of a large-stock portfolio according to Ibbotson data, some counter-argument against a size premium is provided by Berk (1995, 1997).

States as the starting point. Of course, some may argue that the recent strong performance of stock relative to bonds is not sustainable, and therefore that historical data are not indicative of the future. To this end, we assume that the information ratio of a structural bet for stock, which is simply the average risk premium divided by its standard deviation, is 0.3. We further assume that there are twelve other signals, and each has the same information ratio of 0.3.

We then study two scenarios. In the first scenario, alphas of these signals are correlated with each other with a correlation coefficient of 0.25. In the second scenario, the correlations are assumed to be 0.5. These assumptions are made simply for purposes of illustration. The same framework can be applied to other sets of assumptions for similar analysis.

Correlation between Alpha of Signal and Alpha of Structural Bet

Before we begin, we must first compute the correlation between the alpha of a particular signal and the alpha of the structural bet. We use the same notation as in previous chapters. Let x_t be the signal at time t, and y_{t+1} be the subsequent risk premium at time $t+1$. The covariance of the alpha of any one signal, $x_t y_{t+1}$, with the alpha of the structural bet, y_{t+1}, can be computed as

$$Cov\left(x_t y_{t+1}, y_{t+1}\right) = E\left[x_t y_{t+1}^2\right] - E\left[x_t y_{t+1}\right] E\left[y_{t+1}\right] \qquad (6.23)$$

Expanding the terms using moment generating functions of the bivariate normal, we obtain the result:

$$Cov\left(x_t y_{t+1}, y_{t+1}\right) = \rho \sigma_x \sigma_y \mu_y + \mu_x \sigma_y^2 \qquad (6.24)$$

where ρ is the correlation of the signal with the future risk premium, defined as the information coefficient.

To further simplify the analysis, we assume that all signals are unbiased such that $\mu_x = 0$. In this way, all average overweight of stock comes entirely from the structural bet. Given that standard deviations of alphas are by definition their tracking error, the correlation coefficient of the alpha of the signal and the alpha of the structural bet can be computed as

$$Corr\left(x_t y_{t+1}, y_{t+1}\right) = \frac{\rho \sigma_x \sigma_y \mu_y}{TE_x \sigma_y} \qquad (6.25)$$

$$= \frac{\rho \sigma_x \sigma_y}{TE_x} \times \frac{\mu_y}{\sigma_y} \qquad (6.26)$$

Recall from Chapter 4, equation (4.14), that for an unbiased signal, the alpha of volatility capture is given by $\rho \sigma_x \sigma_y$.[4] As a result, we can restate the above equation as

$$Corr\left(x_t y_{t+1}, y_{t+1}\right) = IR_x \times IR_{Structural} \qquad (6.27)$$

---

[4] We ignore the aggressiveness factor for simplicity.

That is, the correlation is equal to the product of the information ratio of the signal and the information ratio of the structural bet. In reality, these results are not exact as their derivation depends on the assumptions of normally distributed signals and risk premium. Jumps in asset returns, such as the global stock crash in October 1987, will certainly skew the statistical distribution to one side. Nevertheless, we maintain the normal distribution assumption for its tractability and wide application.

Combining Structural Bet with Other Signals

Since we assume that all information ratios are 0.3, this gives us a correlation of only 0.09. In fact, with reasonable information ratios, the correlation should range from zero to about 0.25. For simplicity, we just assume that the alphas of the signals and the alpha of the structural bet are uncorrelated. We now have all the necessary assumptions to analyze the effect of a structural bet on the overall information ratio.

We run several experiments. Starting with only one signal, we add a structural bet into the overall portfolio, with aggressiveness factors determined by the OAF based on the covariance matrix and performance statistics assumed. We then repeat the same experiment with two to eleven signals. That is, we first add a structural bet to one signal, then add a structural bet to two signals, and so on until we add a structural bet to eleven signals. We end up with twelve signals altogether, the last one always the structural bet. The maximum information ratio achievable can be computed using equation (6.16).

The results for the case of 0.25 correlation among alphas of signals are plotted in Figure 6.5. We also plot the curve of the maximum information ratio without structural bets for comparison.

It is clear from the figure that, provided that *all aggressiveness factors are determined following the OAF framework, a structural bet always improves the overall information ratio.* The extent of improvement will depend on the other parameters. For example, with two signals and the structural bet, the information ratio is equal to 0.48, compared to the information ratio of 0.42 with three signals. With five signals and the structural bet, the information ratio is improved from 0.49 to 0.56.

The results for the case of 0.5 correlation among alphas of signals are plotted in Figure 6.6 for comparison.

It is important to emphasize that one should not jump to the conclusion that a structural bet will always improve the information ratio. Recall from Chapter 4 that when the size of the structural bet is large enough that it starts to compete away available tracking error from other informative signals, it can actually lead to an information ratio lower than the original unbiased strategy. In fact, the same happens with the OAF approach.

Suppose that the manager is using three signals in making the stock-bond bet, with correlation coefficients of their alphas of 0.25, for example. Since we assume that all signals have the same performance statistics and same information ratio of 0.3, the OAF framework will assign equal weights to all three

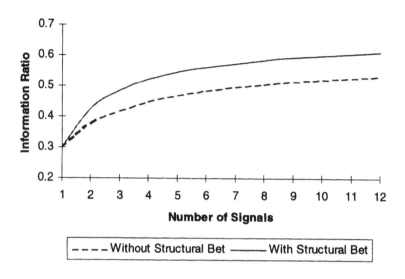

Figure 6.5: Information Ratio with Structural Bet: Correlations $= 0.25$

signals, and the maximum information ratio is computed as 0.42. Now, imagine that the manager knows that a structural bet of a reasonable amount for stock will improve the information ratio. One can use the same OAF framework to determine the range of the reasonable amount as well as the optimal amount of the structural bet, all expressed as optimal aggressiveness factors.

Applying equation (6.13), the vector of optimal aggressiveness factors for a target alpha of 1% is computed as $[0.74, 0.74, 0.74, 1.11]$, and the corresponding maximum information ratio is 0.52. The ratio of the optimal aggressiveness factor of the structural bet to that of the signal is $\frac{1.11}{0.74} = 1.5$. Therefore, we can conclude that the vector $[1, 1, 1, 1.5]$ will also achieve that maximum information ratio of 0.52.

To understand how different degrees of structural bet can affect the information ratio, we fix the aggressiveness factors of all three signals at 1, and vary the aggressiveness factor from -1 to 4. Of course, a negative aggressiveness factor for the structural bet implies that the manager underweights stock intentionally. The resulting information ratios of these combinations of three signals and a structural bet are plotted in Figure 6.7.

Consistent with our previous calculation, the information ratio with a zero aggressiveness factor for a structural bet is equal to 0.42, the maximum information ratio when only the three signals are used. This level of reference is depicted by the dashed horizontal line in the figure. Once again, our results indicate that a negative structural bet always diminishes the information ratio. The more negative the structural bet, the greater the deterioration of the information ratio. The worst scenario for the tactical manager is thus when the

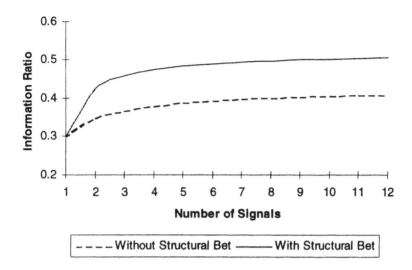

Figure 6.6: Information Ratio with Structural Bet: Correlations $= 0.5$

manager has a negative bias against the higher-return assets.

A positive aggressiveness factor of the structural bet improves the information ratio until the aggressiveness factor is higher than 6. The maximum information ratio of 0.52 is achieved when the aggressiveness factor of the structural bet is 1.5. When it goes beyond the limit of 6, the structural bet leads to a lower information ratio. Again, one can interpret this result as competition of limited tracking error among the signals and the structural bet.

When the weight of the structural bet becomes so dominating that it takes up most of the tracking error available, the benefits of diversification of tracking error diminish. In fact, the curve in Figure 6.7 will approach the asymptote of 0.3 when the aggressiveness factor of the structural bet approaches infinity. In this extreme case, the manager is making the bet completely on the basis of the structural bet, and the resulting information ratio is thus simply the information ratio of the structural bet, namely, 0.3.

In reality, we find that with a reasonable number of signals, performance statistics, and trading ranges, it is most unlikely for a positive structural bet to reduce the information ratio. Typically, the manager will first hit the benchmark constraints of no net short positions well before the structural bet hits its upper limit. Therefore, in most realistic cases, it is safe to conclude that a positive structural bet will improve the information ratio, although the optimal amount will depend on many other parameters in the model.

While our analysis uses the stock-bond pairwise decision as an example, the structural bet issue is most important in the benchmark portfolios with cash. The reason is simple. Since stock and cash are at two extreme ends of the return

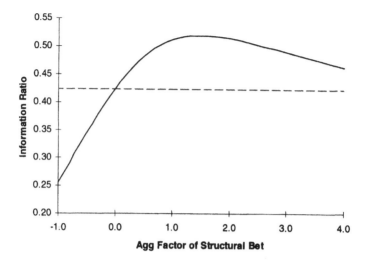

Figure 6.7: Information Ratio of Three Signals with Structural Bet

spectrum, simply overweighting stock should deliver positive alphas over a long period of time.

In order to better visualize this issue, we again implement a strategy that simply overweights stock by 5% against cash. In the sample period from January 1987 through March 1999, this structural bias delivers an annualized alpha of 0.56%, tracking error of 0.77%, information ratio of 0.73, and an impressive hit ratio of 68%. Monthly alpha of the bias is plotted in Figure 6.8.

Of course, probably no managers will implement such a strategy even though it has an impressive performance record. Since there is absolutely no information advantage at all in this strategy, there is no reason for clients to pay managers to implement what effectively is a change in the clients' benchmark portfolios.

In reality, however, this sort of structural bias could be implicitly implemented. The most common examples that we have seen are that managers overweight stocks when expected stock return in excess of cash is positive. Similarly, bonds are overweighted against cash when expected bond return in excess of cash is positive. Typically, these expected excess returns are forecasts from some quantitative models; regression models are the most popular technique. Since these regressions are run with historical data, the positive average historical excess returns of stocks against bonds, stocks against cash, and bonds against cash are all built into these out-of-sample forecasts. Consequently, a structural bias is built into the strategy.

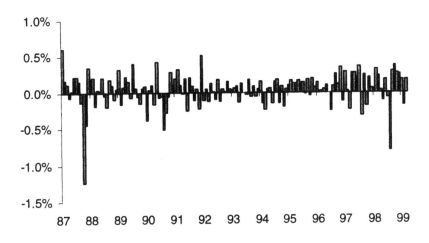

Figure 6.8: Monthly Alpha of a 5% Stock-Cash Structural Bet

6.6 Concluding Remarks

With the objective of maximizing the overall information ratio, we develop a theoretical framework for setting the optimal aggressiveness factors and trading ranges of each asset class in the overall asset allocation portfolio. We articulate the concept of an alpha tracking error efficient frontier, and explain how different pairwise asset allocation strategies can be combined to offer diversification benefits. Using some forward-looking assumptions, we demonstrate that this framework can significantly improve the overall information ratio without any improvement in the quality of information.

We also suggest that the same framework can be applied to pick the optimal mix of asset allocation managers. The results can also be used to shed light on the optimal combination of signals, as well as the number of signals and bets in order to achieve most of the maximum attainable information ratio, given the quality of information. Finally, we use the OAF framework to analyze the effect of a structural bet on the higher-return asset on the overall information ratio.

Chapter 7

Portfolio Construction II: Black-Litterman Approach

7.1 Introduction

Investors make investment decisions by processing the elements in an information set that every piece of information available to the investor at the time decisions are made. Information of different kinds is processed and combined in many different ways. Generally speaking, investors are combining information and blending models and views into a final composite framework that they will use to make informed investment decisions.

In some cases, combinations of models and views are explicit. In predicting returns with regression analysis, for example, several predictive variables are entered into the same regression equation. These predicted returns are then further combined to suggest a portfolio. In other cases, variables may be blended together into one composite indicator. In other cases, while the investors may appear to be using only one model, such as a dividend discount model, different inputs are in fact being combined into one indicator called the dividend discount rate. In short, information processing and combinations of models and views are critical for all investment decisions.

There are far too many different ways of combining information for us to discuss in this book. At the expense of broad coverage, we choose to discuss the Bayesian approach, which has become more popular recently but remains relatively less understood. In particular, this chapter draws heavily on work by Black and Litterman (1991, 1992). The Black-Litterman approach provides an elegant yet practical way to combine views on certain assets with some equilibrium assumptions. The same framework can also be used to combine models. Important insights and potential applications of this framework in tactical asset allocation are discussed.

7.2   A Digression of Bayesian Analysis

Bayesian analysis plays a critical role in the Black-Litterman model. As there is a complete literature on Bayesian methods, we touch only on the important insights behind the Bayes' Law so that we can make intelligent interpretations of the Black-Litterman model.

In classical statistical analysis, parameters of interest are estimated according to a set of observed data. The Bayesian approach, however, proposes that views about the state of the world are subjective. Instead of estimating parameters as if they were fixed, we should use recently observed data to constantly update and sharpen our subjective prior beliefs about the current state.

The centerpiece driving all Bayesian methods is Bayes' Law, which states that

$$\Pr(A|B) = \frac{\Pr(B|A)\Pr(A)}{\Pr(B)} \tag{7.1}$$

In words, Bayes' Law states that the conditional probability of state A, given state B, is equal to the product of the conditional probability of state B, given state A, and the probability of state A, divided by the probability of state B.

To put Bayes' Law in an applicable format, suppose A denotes expected return to be estimated, and B denotes the data observed. We rewrite Bayes' Law as

$$\Pr(E[R]|\text{data}) = \frac{\Pr(\text{data}|E[R])\Pr(E[R])}{\Pr(\text{data})} \tag{7.2}$$

The first term in the numerator of the right-hand side is the joint distribution of the observed data, given the expected return. The second term is the prior belief, or subjective views, on expected return. The product of these two terms is then scaled by the probability of the observed data to obtain the left-hand side, which is known as the posterior density of expected return. This posterior is thus a mixture of the prior beliefs and the current state of the world based on the observed data.

In this way, the observed data are used to refine the subjective views on expected return. When new subsequent data are available, the current posterior becomes the next prior beliefs, which will be used to adjust the density function of the expected return, given the new data, and so on. This sequential update of density function is applied in the Black-Litterman approach in that an investor's views about expected returns are used to adjust the refinement of expected returns away from the equilibrium.

7.3   Black-Litterman Approach

Typical quantitative portfolio optimization tools for asset allocation are known to produce badly behaved portfolios. That is, the outputs are extremely sensitive to small changes in the inputs, or the resulting portfolios are close to corner solutions. Michaud (1989, 1998) attributes these results to the error-maximization nature of an optimizer, which has the effect of significantly over-weighting assets with positive errors in their expected returns. The elegant Black-Litterman model was originally developed to solve this problem and to make quantitative tools more practical for asset allocation.

As we will show, the insights behind their Bayesian approach in combining views with market equilibrium can be equally applicable in combining models and views. We discuss this approach, interpret the results, and propose potential applications in tactical asset allocation.

7.3.1   The Model

Black and Litterman (1991, 1992) assert that the only meaningful set of equilibrium returns is the set of expected returns that would clear the market if all investors have identical views. Let us further assume that the capital asset pricing model (CAPM) holds in general; it implies that the weights based on the market capitalization of the assets are the optimal portfolio weights under a CAPM equilibrium.

Under these conditions, and assuming a relative risk aversion coefficient, the vector of equilibrium returns can be backed out from the optimal market portfolio holding equation implied by the CAPM equilibrium, such as in Ingersoll (1987) and Merton (1990). To be consistent with the study by Black and Litterman (1992), we denote this $n \times 1$ CAPM-equilibrium vector of returns by Π.[1] Note that the vector of equilibrium returns, $\overline{\mathbf{R}}$, in previous chapters denotes the more general case in that it can be derived from any other means, such as a vector of forward-looking assumptions, or based on moving averages following a filtering rule discussed in Chapter 5.

In order to specify the equilibrium distribution of expected returns, $E[\mathbf{R}]$, we also need an estimate of its covariance matrix. While the covariance matrix can be conditional on any information set, for the sake of simplification, Black and Litterman assume that it is proportional to the covariance matrix of historical return by a multiple of τ. Since uncertainty of the mean should be much lower than the uncertainly of the variable, the value of τ should be close to zero.

By now, we have a complete specification of the equilibrium distribution of expected returns as

$$E[\mathbf{R}] \sim N(\Pi, \tau\Omega) \tag{7.3}$$

where Ω is an $n \times n$ covariance matrix of realized historical returns, and $E[\mathbf{R}]$ is a $n \times 1$ vector of expected returns.[2]

The most elegant and innovative part of the model is the way it combines uncertain views about expected returns with the equilibrium. Assume the in-

---

[1] In Black and Litterman (1992), Π actually stands for the vector of the equilibrium risk premium relative to the return of a risk-free asset. We ignore this detail here, which does not alter any of our conclusions.

[2] See Litterman and Winkelmann (1998) for examples of investment industry practice in estimating covariance matrices.

vestor has no views on expected returns of any assets at all. In this case, the investor should simply hold the market portfolio, which is the equilibrium state at which supply is equal to demand. When the investor has some views about expected returns, the difficult task is to combine these views with the market equilibrium in a coherent framework.

Of course, to be realistic, there is some degree of uncertainty about an investor's views. Therefore, both sources of information, the equilibrium expected returns and the views, are expressed as probability distributions. The relative weights put on the equilibrium versus the views then depend on the investor's relative degree of confidence in these sources of information.

If the investor is highly uncertain about the views, the final portfolio compositions should depend more on the equilibrium. If the investor is very confident in the views, the final portfolio compositions will be driven more by the views, and the portfolio weights will thus deviate more from the equilibrium market portfolio.

To implement this idea, the views must first be expressed as a probability distribution. Assume the investor has k different views on linear combinations of expected returns of the n assets. It is assumed that these views can be represented by the matrix formula:

$$\mathbf{P}E\left[\mathbf{R}\right] = \mathbf{V} + \mathbf{e} \tag{7.4}$$

where $\mathbf{P}$ is a $k \times n$ matrix, $\mathbf{V}$ is a $k \times 1$ vector, and $\mathbf{e}$ is also a $k \times 1$ vector, which represents the error terms of views.

The first view is represented as a linear combination of expected returns denoted by the first row of $\mathbf{P}$. The value of this linear combination is given by the first element of $\mathbf{V}$, plus an error as the first element of $\mathbf{e}$. As a result, the degree of uncertainty of a particular view is measured by the standard deviation of the corresponding error term. The higher the standard deviation of the error term, the more uncertain (less confident) the investor on the view. The covariance matrix of the error terms is denoted by $\boldsymbol{\xi}$. When the views represent independent draws from the future returns distribution, or when the deviations of expected returns from the means of the distribution representing each view are independent, $\boldsymbol{\xi}$ is a diagonal matrix with zeros in all off-diagonal elements.

For purposes of illustration, consider a simple case with three assets denoted as asset 1, asset 2, and asset 3. The investor has the views that asset 1 will outperform asset 2 by 2%, while asset 3 will outperform asset 2 by 1%. In this case, $k = 2$, and these two views can be represented in matrix form as

$$\begin{pmatrix} 1 & -1 & 0 \\ 0 & -1 & 1 \end{pmatrix} \begin{pmatrix} E\left[R_1\right] \\ E\left[R_2\right] \\ E\left[R_3\right] \end{pmatrix} = \begin{pmatrix} 2\% \\ 1\% \end{pmatrix} + \begin{pmatrix} e_1 \\ e_2 \end{pmatrix} \tag{7.5}$$

where the relative values of the standard deviations of the elements in the error vector would indicate the relative degree of confidence in these views.

After the equilibrium distribution of expected return in equation (7.3) and the views in equation (7.4) are specified, we are ready to derive the formula to combine these two sources of information.

Certain Views

When there is 100% confidence in the views, the standard deviations of all the error terms in views are zero, and thus they are excluded. In this case, we can compute the distribution of expected returns conditional on the equilibrium and views as the solution to the problem:

$$\min_{E[\mathbf{R}]} (E[\mathbf{R}] - \Pi)' \tau\Omega (E[\mathbf{R}] - \Pi)$$

$$\text{subject to } \mathbf{P}E[\mathbf{R}] = \mathbf{V}$$

This can be interpreted as a least-squares minimization problem, in which the sum of squares of deviations of expected returns from the vector of equilibrium, $(E[\mathbf{R}] - \Pi)$, weighted by the covariance matrix, $\tau\Omega$, is minimized. Skipping the details of the matrix algebra, we solve the problem by the standard Lagrangian method to get the solution

$$\text{Mean of } E[\mathbf{R}] = \Pi + \tau\Omega\mathbf{P}' \left(\mathbf{P}\tau\Omega\mathbf{P}'\right)^{-1} (\mathbf{V} - \mathbf{P}\Pi) \tag{7.6}$$

Uncertain Views

In the more realistic case when the investor is not 100% confident in the views, the standard deviations of the error vector $\mathbf{e}$ will be non-zero. The conditional distribution of expected returns can be derived on the basis of direct application of Bayes' Law. In effect, the prior beliefs about the returns distribution represented by the views are used to adjust the equilibrium distribution of returns. Skipping all the details in using the conjugate prior to derive the probability density function of the expected returns, it can be shown that the conditional distribution of $E[\mathbf{R}]$ is a normal with[3]

$$\text{Mean of } E[\mathbf{R}] = \left[\left(\tau\Omega\boldsymbol{\xi}^{-1}\right)^{-1} + \mathbf{P}'\mathbf{P}\right]^{-1} \left[\left(\tau\Omega\right)^{-1}\boldsymbol{\xi}\Pi + \mathbf{P}'\mathbf{V}\right] \tag{7.7}$$

Some additional matrix algebra is required in order to get the exact expression in the original Black and Litterman study, which is written as

$$\text{Mean of } E[\mathbf{R}] = \left[\left(\tau\Omega\right)^{-1} + \mathbf{P}'\boldsymbol{\xi}^{-1}\mathbf{P}\right]^{-1} \left[\left(\tau\Omega\right)^{-1}\Pi + \mathbf{P}'\boldsymbol{\xi}^{-1}\mathbf{V}\right] \tag{7.8}$$

As investor confidence in the views approaches 100%, it can be shown that, in the limit, the solution in equation (7.8) will approach the solution for the 100% confidence case given by equation (7.6).

---

[3] Black and Litterman (1992) suggest that the solution can be derived by the "mixed estimation" of Theil (1971). Davidson and MacKinnon (1993) expand Theil's method. An easier way is to treat the problem as a Bayesian estimation of a regression model with the expected returns as the coefficients to be estimated, and the investor's views used as priors to update the density function. See Hamilton (1994) for examples of Bayesian regressions. In fact, this is the approach outlined in the appendix of Black and Litterman (1992), although many readers may not find this obvious.

7.3.2 Interpretations

The solution in equation (7.8) involves complicated matrix algebra. Neverthe-less, there are some simple and important insights embedded in this solution.

- If the investor has no particular views on expected returns, the equilibrium distribution of returns should be used, which will lead to holding the market portfolio as implied by the CAPM equilibrium.[4]

- Views are expressed in relative terms, such as "asset 1 will outperform as-set 2 by 2%." This is closer to the way investors actually compare different assets when they make investment decisions. This is also consistent with the results derived in Chapter 2 that bets have a pairwise structure in that one asset is compared to all other assets in the investment universe.

- Even if the investor does not have an explicit view on a particular asset, the fact that all assets are correlated to some extent means that the investor is expressing some implicit views on this asset, based on the investor's views on other assets and the covariance matrix of these assets. This result comes from the matrix multiplications among $\mathbf{P}$, $\tau\Omega$, and $\boldsymbol{\xi}$, which denote the views expressed as linear combinations of expected returns, the covariance matrix of equilibrium expected returns, and the covariance matrix of views. For example, the investor expects asset 1 to outperform asset 2. If asset 3 has a very high positive correlation with asset 1, its expected return must also be raised through its highly positive covariance with asset 1, even though the investor has never given an explicit view on asset 3. It is this characteristic that makes the Black-Litterman model a much more practical model to use than typical mean-variance optimizers. While the latter simply computes the final optimized portfolio weights based on inputs with errors, the Black-Litterman model "spreads out" the errors of the inputs to all others through the covariance matrices of returns and views so that the error-maximization problem of an optimizer is largely mitigated.[5] This redistribution of errors is made to happen in a controlled fashion, consistent with the way these assets move with one another as well as the investor's relative confidence about its views.

7.3.3 A Weighted Average of Equilibrium and Views

While the Black-Litterman model in equation (7.8) can be applied directly, exactly how are the equilibrium and the views combined? Under what conditions will the model put more weight on equilibrium, or the views? We must take another look at equation (7.8) in order to dig out the most illuminating insights behind this matrix formula.

---

[4] An easy way to see this is to substitute an $n \times n$ matrix of zero for $\mathbf{P}$ in equation (7.8).
[5] See Michaud (1998) for taming optimizers according to a statistical perspective.

For reasons that will become clear, we focus on the expression in the second set of brackets in equation (7.8), and reexpress it as

$$\left[(\tau\Omega)^{-1}\,\Pi + \left(\mathbf{P}'\boldsymbol{\xi}^{-1}\mathbf{P}\right)\left(\mathbf{P}'\mathbf{P}\right)^{-1}\mathbf{P}'\mathbf{V} \right] \tag{7.9}$$

The important point to be made here is on the $n \times 1$ vector, $(\mathbf{P}'\mathbf{P})^{-1}\,\mathbf{P}'\mathbf{V}$. If we rearrange equation (7.4) into

$$\mathbf{V} = \mathbf{P}E\left[\mathbf{R}\right] + \mathbf{e}^* \tag{7.10}$$

where $\mathbf{e}^*$ is just a redefined error vector such that $\mathbf{e}^* = -\mathbf{e}$, we may interpret the specification of the investor's views as a regression of $\mathbf{V}$ on $\mathbf{P}$ so that $E\left[\mathbf{R}\right]$ is the vector of coefficients to be estimated.[6] In this framework of analysis, it becomes obvious that the vector $(\mathbf{P}'\mathbf{P})^{-1}\,\mathbf{P}'\mathbf{V}$ can be interpreted as the least-squares estimate of expected returns, $E\left[\mathbf{R}\right]$, according to the investor's views.[7] That is:

$$(\mathbf{P}'\mathbf{P})^{-1}\,\mathbf{P}'\mathbf{V} = \widehat{E\left[\mathbf{R}\right]} \tag{7.11}$$

where the hat denotes that the variable is a least-squares estimate.

Putting all the pieces together, the Black-Litterman model can now be rewritten as

$$\text{Mean of } E\left[\mathbf{R}\right] = \left[(\tau\Omega)^{-1} + \mathbf{P}'\boldsymbol{\xi}^{-1}\mathbf{P}\right]^{-1}\left[(\tau\Omega)^{-1}\,\Pi + \left(\mathbf{P}'\boldsymbol{\xi}^{-1}\mathbf{P}\right)\widehat{E\left[\mathbf{R}\right]}\right] \tag{7.12}$$

Equation (7.12) makes it easier to understand how the Black-Litterman model combines equilibrium and views. As the expression in the first set of brackets is a common multiplier for both terms in the second bracket, it can be ignored for the time being. Focusing on the expression in the second set of brackets, one can see that the Black-Litterman model is in fact a simple weighted average of equilibrium and views, with the weights of $(\tau\Omega)^{-1}$ and $\left(\mathbf{P}'\boldsymbol{\xi}^{-1}\mathbf{P}\right)$, respectively. Since these weights are vectors instead of scalars, comparison between them must be on an element-to-element basis. A general conclusion can nevertheless be drawn based on the forms of these vector weights.

If the distribution of expected return around the equilibrium is tight, that is, $\tau\Omega$ is small, $(\tau\Omega)^{-1}$ will be large, and therefore more weight will be put on the equilibrium Π. If the investor is confident in the views, that is, $\boldsymbol{\xi}$ is small so that $\left(\mathbf{P}'\boldsymbol{\xi}^{-1}\mathbf{P}\right)$ is large, more weight will then be put on the views, represented by $\widehat{E\left[\mathbf{R}\right]}$.

---

[6] Note that this interpretation is not exactly correct. When the number of views that the investor has is fewer than the number of assets, that is, $k < n$, this is the same as there being more parameters to be estimated than the number of observations in a regression. In this case, the matrix $\mathbf{P}'\mathbf{P}$ is non-invertible.

[7] Here we make a direct application of the well-known "normal equation" in ordinary-least squares estimation, which states that the ordinary least-squares estimate of parameters in a regression of $\mathbf{Y} = \mathbf{X}'\boldsymbol{\beta} + \boldsymbol{\varepsilon}$ is equal to $(\mathbf{X}'\mathbf{X})^{-1}\,\mathbf{X}'\mathbf{Y}$. See Davidson and MacKinnon (1993), or any introductory text in econometrics.

In short, the Black-Litterman model is a simple weighted average of equilibrium and views, where the relative weights are determined by the perceived degree of dispersion of expected returns from equilibrium and the confidence in views.

7.4   Applications in Tactical Asset Allocation

While the original Black-Litterman model assumes that the CAPM has to hold in that the equilibrium distribution of returns can be backed out from market portfolio weights, this assumption does not affect the concepts and the ultimate solution in equation (7.8) at all. A straightforward application of the model in tactical asset allocation is to replace the CAPM equilibrium vector of returns, Π, in equation (7.8) by the vector of expected returns that makes the investor neutral in making any tactical bets. In other words, the vector of equilibrium returns that makes the investor hold the strategic benchmark portfolio should be used in place of Π. To be consistent with the notation in previous chapters, we denote this vector of equilibrium by $\overline{\mathbf{R}}$.

If the investor does not have any views on the expected returns of assets, by definition, no tactical bets are made, and the investor should simply hold the benchmark portfolio. If the investor has some views that can be expressed as linear combinations of expected returns in the form of equation (7.4), the final portfolio positions can be determined directly by equation (7.8).

Alternatively, the Black-Litterman model can be used to combine different models. For example, dividend discount models are widely used to estimate expected returns for stocks in the investment industry. Or, there are other signals, such as technical indicators, that cannot be directly incorporated into these valuation models. In this way, one might use the Black-Litterman model to derive a set of composite signals. To do so, expected returns from dividend discount models can be treated as the neutral points so that, when no technical indicators are used, the tactical bets are determined simply by the dividend discount models. When technical indicators are used, the final technical bets will deviate from those recommended by the dividend discount models alone, with the degree of deviation depending on the relative confidence in these indicators as well as the covariance matrix. Conceptually, the composite signals are determined by equation (7.12) as a weighted average of dividend discount models and technical indicators.

7.5   Implied Tactical Trading Rule

According to standard financial theory texts such as Ingersoll (1987), Merton (1990), and Duffie (1996), the optimal portfolio for a risk-averse investor is a weighted average of the minimum-variance portfolio and a second portfolio whose vector of weights is proportional to $\Omega^{-1} E[\mathbf{R}]$. This same result is also derived in Chapter 2, equation (2.27). For simplicity, we can ignore the proportionality constant and just write the optimal portfolio in an equivalent form as in equation (2.29) where ω_g is the global minimum variance portfolio, and γ denotes the relative risk aversion coefficient.

When the investor does not have any views on expected returns and makes no tactical bets, the optimal portfolio will be just the benchmark portfolio given by

$$\omega^*_{bench} = \omega_g + \frac{\Omega^{-1}}{\gamma}\left(\overline{\mathbf{R}} - 1\frac{1'\Omega^{-1}\overline{\mathbf{R}}}{1'\Omega^{-1}1}\right) \tag{7.13}$$

where ω^*_{bench} denotes the benchmark portfolio.

When the investor uses the Black-Litterman model in equation (7.12) to derive a revised expected return forecast, however, the optimal portfolio becomes

$$\omega^*_{BL} = \omega_g + \frac{\Omega^{-1}}{\gamma}\left(E\left[\mathbf{R}\right] - 1\frac{1'\Omega^{-1}E\left[\mathbf{R}\right]}{1'\Omega^{-1}1}\right) \tag{7.14}$$

where ω^*_{BL} denotes the optimal portfolio applying the Black-Litterman model. Therefore, the vector of tactical bets, **Bet**, is given by

$$\mathbf{Bet} = \omega^*_{BL} - \omega^*_{bench} \tag{7.15}$$

$$= \frac{\Omega^{-1}}{\gamma}\left((E\left[\mathbf{R}\right] - \overline{\mathbf{R}}) - 1\frac{1'\Omega^{-1}\left(E\left[\mathbf{R}\right] - \overline{\mathbf{R}}\right)}{1'\Omega^{-1}1}\right) \tag{7.16}$$

where $E\left[\mathbf{R}\right]$ is given by equation (7.12).

With all this matrix algebra, we finally establish a workable formula for tactical bets as expressed in equation (7.15). In the end, the tactical trading rule implied by the Black-Litterman model is similar to the trading rule under the total return/total risk framework discussed in Chapter 2. That is, tactical bets are triggered by deviations of expected returns from equilibrium.

There is one main difference that distinguishes the Black-Litterman model from the traditional trading rule. When the full expression of $E\left[\mathbf{R}\right]$ in equation (7.12) is substituted into equation (7.15), it becomes obvious that other than incorporating the covariance matrix of the asset returns, the way views are formed as well as the covariance matrix of these views also enter into this matrix through $\mathbf{P}$ and ξ^{-1}. Since aggressiveness factors are more for the purpose of risk control, the Black-Litterman model has a different view on what risks are important in making tactical bets. It assumes that those views in which one has less confidence, or higher variances in the diagonal of the matrix ξ, are risky, and therefore, the degree of aggressiveness of the corresponding bets should be lower.

7.6 Concluding Remarks

The Black-Litterman model is designed to be used for combining equilibrium with mostly subjective views about returns. There are many degrees of freedom in its implementation, and very often the framework is used in an iterative process until the investor feels that the right portfolio balance has been achieved. Examples of its implementation is documented in Bevan and Winkelmann (1998) and He and Litterman (1999). There is no rule of thumb for putting the model to work. Perhaps it is this flexibility that makes the Black-Litterman model so attractable to different investors with different situations.

Chapter 8

Epilogue on Portfolio Construction

In Chapters 6 and 7, we discuss two different tools for tactical asset allocation portfolio construction: the maximizing information ratio optimal aggressiveness factors approach, and the Black-Litterman equilibrium approach. These by no means represent a comprehensive coverage of portfolio construction.

For instance, strict application of the OAF approach may have some disadvantage. A good example is the global stock crash in 1987. Consider two signals for the stock-bond bet. One signal is a valuation signal, and the other one is a momentum signal that simply buys the winner and sells the loser. In early 1987, value signals would have done poorly, while momentum signals would have done well. Imagine now that the OAF framework was applied to determine relative weightings of these two signals near the end of September 1987. It is highly likely that a relatively large weight would have been assigned to the momentum signal, and a small, if not negative, weight to the valuation signal. As a result, one might have underweighted the valuation signal precisely when it was needed the most, in October 1987.

Of course, sudden jumps like this crash are rare events, but the possibility of their occurrence cannot be ruled out. In real-life application, it is useful to add some constraints to the optimizer to help maintain the balance. For example, one might use a longer sample period to determine the optimal mix of signals. Using this as the long-term optimal mix, more recent periods of performance of the signals can then be used as inputs into the optimizer so as to constrain the resulting mix to be within a certain band of the long-term optimal mix of signals. The drawback of this approach is that an analytical solution is no longer available. Instead, the problem must be solved numerically. Alternatively, if the TAA manager prefers to be labeled as a valuation- and fundamentals- driven manager, a constraint to weight the valuation signal at at least 50% can be used.

While the Black-Litterman model provides an elegant platform to combine investment insights with equilibrium or the benchmark portfolio, some other risk control issues are not incorporated. For example, one may want to impose an upper bound of 30% of tracking error risk from any particular bet so as to maintain a balance on sources of risks. In practice, other constraints are usually added to the optimizer that uses the vector of expected returns as output from the Black-Litterman model. Furthermore, the Black-Litterman model is not designed to maximize the information ratio, which is one of the most dominating performance evaluation measures in the asset allocation industry.

In short, there is no rule of thumb for the optimal portfolio construction process. Most investors or managers want the freedom to apply different analytical tools.

Bibliography

[1] Arnott, Robert, and Frank J. Fabozzi, *Asset Allocation: A Handbook of Portfolio Policies, Strategies and Tactics*, 1988, Probus, Chicago, Illinois.

[2] Arnott, Robert, and Todd Miller, "Surprise! TAA Can Work in Quiet Markets," *Journal of Investing*, Fall 1997, pp. 33-45.

[3] Banz, R.W., "The Relationship between Return and Market Value of Common Stocks," *Journal of Financial Economics*, 1981, pp. 3-18.

[4] Barberis, Nicholas, "Investing for the Long Run When Returns are Predictable," *Journal of Finance*, February 2000, pp. 225-264.

[5] Berk, Jonathan B., "A Critique of Size-Related Anomalies," *Review of Financial Studies*, 1995, Vol.8 No. 2, pp. 275-286.

[6] Berk, Jonathan B., "Does Size Really Matter," *Financial Analysts Journal*, September/October 1997, pp. 12-18.

[7] Bevan, Andrew, and Kurt Winkelmann, "Using the Black-Litterman Global Asset Allocation Model: Three Years of Practical Experience," June 1998, Goldman Sachs working paper.

[8] Black, Fischer, and Robert Jones, "Simplifying Portfolio Insurance," *Journal of Portfolio Management*, Fall 1987, pp. 48-51.

[9] Black, Fischer, and Robert Litterman, "Asset Allocation: Combining Investors Views with Market Equilibrium," *Journal of Fixed Income*, September 1991, pp. 7-18.

[10] Black, Fischer, and Robert Litterman, "Global Portfolio Optimization," *Financial Analysts Journal*, September/October 1992, pp. 28-43.

[11] Black, Fischer, and André Perold, "Theory of Constant Proportion Portfolio Insurance," *Journal of Economic Dynamics and Control*, Vol. 16, 1992, pp. 403-426.

[12] Black, Fischer, and Myron Scholes, "The Pricing of Options and Corporate Liabilities," *Journal of Political Economy*, May/June 1973, pp. 637-654.

[13] Bossaerts, Peter, and Pierre Hillion, "Implementing Statistical Criteria to Select Return Forecasting Models: What Do We Learn?" *Review of Financial Studies*, Summer 1999, pp. 405-428.

[14] Boudoukh, Jacob, "Can Market-Timers Time Markets? Evidence on the Predictability of Stock Returns from Asset Allocation Funds" November 1994, working paper, Stern School of Business, New York University.

[15] Brandt, Michael W., "Estimating Portfolio and Consumption Choice: A Conditional Euler Equations Approach," *Journal of Finance*, October 1999, pp. 1609-1645.

[16] Breen, William, Lawrence R. Glosten, and Ravi Jagannathan, "Economic Significance of Predictable Variations in Stock Index Returns," *Journal of Finance*, December 1989, pp. 1177-1189.

[17] Brennan, Michael J., Eduardo S. Schwartz, and Ronald Lagnado, "Strategic Asset Allocation," *Journal of Economic Dynamics and Control*, 1997, pp. 1377-1403.

[18] Brinson, Gary P., L. Randolph Hood, and Gilbert L. Beebower, "Determinants of Portfolio Performance," *Financial Analysts Journal*, July/August 1986, pp. 39-44.

[19] Brinson, Gary P., Brian D. Singer and Gilbert L. Beebower, "Determinants of Portfolio Performance II: An Update," *Financial Analysts Journal*, May/June 1991, pp. 40-48.

[20] Britten-Jones, Mark, "The Sampling Error in Estimates of Mean-Variance Efficient Portfolio Weights" *Journal of Finance*, April 1999, pp. 655-672.

[21] Brocato, Joe, and P.R. Chandy, "Does Market Timing Really Work in the Real World?" *Journal of Portfolio Management*, Winter 1994, pp. 39-44.

[22] Campbell, John Y., "A Variance Decomposition for Stock Returns," *Economic Journal*, March 1991, pp. 157-179.

[23] Campbell, John Y., Andrew W. Lo, and A. Craig MacKinlay, *The Econometrics of Financial Markets*, 1997, Princeton University Press, Princeton, New Jersey.

[24] Campbell, John Y., and Luis M. Viceira, "Consumption and Portfolio Decisions when Expected Returns are Time Varying," 1999, forthcoming in the *Quarterly Journal of Economics*.

[25] Campbell, John Y., Joao Cocco, Francisco Gomes, Pascal J. Maenhout, and Luis M. Viceira, "Stock Market Mean Reversion and the Optimal Equity Allocation," 1998, working paper, Department of Economics, Harvard University.

[26] Campbell, John Y., and John H. Cochrane, "By Force of Habit: A Consumption-Based Explanation of Aggregate Stock Market Behavior," April 1999, *Journal of Political Economy*, pp. 205-251.

[27] Chacko, George, and Luis M. Viceira, "Dynamic Consumption and Portfolio Choice with Stochastic Volatility in Incomplete Markets," 1999, working paper, Graduate School of Business Administration, Harvard University.

[28] Chen, Carl R., Anthony Chan, and Nancy J. Mohan, "Asset Allocator Managers' Investment Performance," *Journal of Fixed Income*, December 1993, pp. 46-53.

[29] Clarke, Roger G., "Tactical Asset Allocation as a Stand-Alone Asset," *Derivatives Quarterly*, Spring 1997, pp. 55-59.

[30] Clarke, Roger G., Michael T. FitzGerald, Phillip Berent, and Meir Statman, "Market Timing with Imperfect Information," *Financial Analysts Journal*, November/December 1989, pp. 27-36.

[31] Clarke, Roger G., Michael T. FitzGerald, Phillip Berent, and Meir Statman, "Required Accuracy for Successful Asset Allocation," *Journal of Portfolio Management*, Fall 1990, pp. 12-19.

[32] Clarke, Roger G., Michael T. FitzGerald, Phillip Berent, and Meir Statman, "Diversifying Among Asset Allocators," *Journal of Portfolio Management*, Spring 1990, pp. 9-14.

[33] Conrad, Jennifer, and Gautam Kaul, "An Anatomy of Trading Strategies," *Review of Financial Studies*, Fall 1998, pp. 489-519.

[34] Cox, John, and Chi-Fu Huang, "Optimal Consumption and Portfolio Policies When Asset Prices Follow a Diffusion Process," *Journal of Economic Theory*, October 1989, pp. 33-83.

[35] Cumby, Robert E., and David M. Modest, "Testing for Market Timing Ability: A Framework for Forecast Evaluation," *Journal of Financial Economics*, 1987, pp. 169-190.

[36] Das, Sanjiv Ranjan, and Rangarajan K. Sundaram, "Of Smiles and Smirks: A Term-Structure Perspective," June 1999, *Journal of Financial and Quantitative Analysis*, pp. 211-240.

[37] Davidson, Russell, and James G. MacKinnon, *Estimation and Inference in Econometrics*, 1993, Oxford University Press, London.

[38] Dothan, Michael, *Prices in Financial Markets*, 1990, Oxford University Press, New York, New York.

[39] Duffie, Darrell, *Dynamic Asset Pricing Theory*, 2nd edition, 1996, Princeton University Press, Princeton, New Jersey.

[40] Erb, Claude B., Campbell R. Harvey, and Tadas E. Viskanta, "Forecasting International Equity Correlations," *Financial Analysts Journal*, November/December 1994, pp. 32-45.

[41] Fama, Eugene, "Stock Return, Real Activity, Inflation, and Money," *American Economic Review*, 1981, vol. 71, pp. 545-565.

[42] Fama, Eugene, and Kenneth French, "Permanent and Temporary Components of Stock Prices," *Journal of Political Economy*, 1988, vol. 96 no. 2 pp. 246-273.

[43] Fama, Eugene, and Kenneth French, "Busniess Conditions and Expected Returns on Stocks and Bonds," *Journal of Financial Economics*, 1989, vol. 25 no. 1 pp. 23-50.

[44] Fama, Eugene, and Kenneth French, "Value versus Growth: The International Evidence," *Journal of Finance*, December 1998, pp. 1975-1999.

[45] Fama, Eugene, and William Schwert, "Asset Returns and Inflation," *Journal of Financial Economics*, 1977, vol. 5, pp. 115-146.

[46] Ferson, Wayne E., and Campbell R. Harvey, "The Risk and Predictability of International Equity Returns," *Review of Financial Studies*, 1993, vol. 6 no. 3 pp. 527-566.

[47] Froot, Kenneth A., "Short Rates and Expected Asset Returns," *NBER working paper* #3247, 1990.

[48] Geske, Robert L., and Richard Roll, "The Monetary and Fiscal Linkage between Stock Returns and Inflation," *Journal of Finance*, 1983, pp. 1-33.

[49] Gibbons, Michael R., Stephen A. Ross, and Jay Shanken, "A Test of the Efficiency of a Given Portfolio," *Econometrica*, 1989, pp. 1121-1152.

[50] Goodwin, Thomas H., "The Information Ratio," *Financial Analysts Journal*, July/August 1998, pp. 34-43.

[51] Granito, Michael R., "Investment Rules and the Ergodic Hypothesis," *Journal of Portfolio Management*, Fall 1986, pp. 50-58.

[52] Granito, Michael R., "The Secret of Duration Averaging," in *New Developments in Fixed Income Markets*, Frank J. Fabozzi, editor, 1987, Dow Jones-Irwin, Homewood, Illinois.

[53] Grinold, Richard C., "The Fundamental Law of Active Management," *Journal of Portfolio Management*, Spring 1989, pp. 30-37.

[54] Grinold, Richard C., "Alpha is Volatility Times IC Times Score," *Journal of Portfolio Management*, Summer 1994, pp. 9-16.

[55] Grinold, Richard C., and Ronald N. Kahn, *Active Portfolio Management*, 1995, Irwin, Chicago, Illinois.

[56] Hamilton, James D., *Time Series Analysis*, 1994, Princeton University Press, Princeton, New Jersey.

[57] Harvey, Campbell R., and Akhtar Siddique, "Conditional Skewness in Asset Pricing Tests," 2000, forthcoming in *Journal of Finance*.

[58] Harvey, Campbell R., and Akhtar Siddique, "Autoregressive Conditional Skewness," December 1999, *Journal of Financial and Quantitative Analysis*, pp. 465-488.

[59] He, Guangliang, and Robert Litterman, "The Intuition Behind Black-Litterman Model Portfolios," 1999, Goldman Sachs Quantitative Resources Group working paper.

[60] Henriksson, Roy D., and Robert C. Merton, "On Market Timing and Investment Performance II: Statistical Procedures for Evaluating Forecasting Skills," *Journal of Business*, 1981, pp. 513-534.

[61] Hensel, Chris R., D. Don Ezra, and John H. Ilkiw, "The Importance of the Asset Allocation Decision," *Financial Analysts Journal*, July/August 1991, pp. 65-72.

[62] Ilmanen, Antti, "Time-Varying Expected Returns in International Bond Markets," *Journal of Finance*, June 1995, pp. 481-506.

[63] Ingersoll, Jonathan E. Jr., *Theory of Financial Decision Making*, 1987, Rowman & Littlefield, Totowa, New Jersey.

[64] Jensen, Michael C., "Risk, The Pricing of Capital Assets, and the Evaluation of Investment Portfolios," *Journal of Business*, 1969, vol. 42 (2), pp. 167-247.

[65] Kandel, Shmuel, and Robert F. Stambaugh, "On The Predictability of Stock Returns: An Asset Allocation Perspective," *Journal of Finance*, June 1996, pp. 385-424.

[66] Kaul, Gautam, "Monetary Regimes and the Relation between Stock Returns and Inflationary Expectations," *Journal of Financial and Quantitative Analysis*, 1990, vol. 25, pp. 307-321.

[67] Kaul, Gautam, "Stock Returns and Inflation: The Role of the Monetary Sector," *Journal of Financial Economics*, 1987, vol. 18, pp. 253-276.

[68] Kendall, M.G., and A. Stuart, *The Advanced Theory of Statistics, Volume I*, 1977, 4th edition, Charles Griffin, London.

[69] Kim. Tong Suk, and Edward Omberg, "Dynamic Nonmyopic Portfolio Behavior," *Review of Financial Studies* 9, 1996, pp. 141-161.

[70] Lederman, Jess, and Robert A. Klein (eds.), *Global Asset Allocation: Techniques for Optimizing Portfolio Management*, 1994, Wiley, New York, New York.

[71] Lee, Wai, "Mean-Variance Analysis of Total-Return/Total Risk, Active-Return/Active Risk, and Tactical Asset Allocation," 1997a, J.P. Morgan Investment Management, working paper.

[72] Lee, Wai, "Optimal Aggressiveness Factors and Trading Ranges in Asset Allocation," 1997b, J.P. Morgan Investment Management, working paper.

[73] Lee, Wai, "Theory of Signal Filtering," 1997c, J.P. Morgan Investment Management, working paper.

[74] Lee, Wai, "Market Timing and Short-Term Interest Rates," *Journal of Portfolio Management*, Spring 1997d, pp. 35-46.

[75] Lee, Wai, "Return and Risk Characteristics of Tactical Asset Allocation Under Imperfect Information," *Journal of Portfolio Management*, Fall 1998, pp. 61-70.

[76] Litterman, Robert, and Kurt Winkelmann, "Estimating Covariance Matrices," 1998, Goldman Sachs working paper.

[77] Lo, Andrew (eds.), *Market Efficiency: Stock Market Behaviour in Theory and Practice*, 1997, Edward Elgar Publishing, Ltd., London.

[78] MacBeth, James D., and David C. Emanuel, "Tactical Asset Allocation: Pros and Cons," *Financial Analysts Journal*, November/December 1993, pp. 30-43.

[79] Merton, Robert C., "Lifetime Portfolio Selection Under Uncertainty: The Continuous-Time Case," *Review of Economics and Statistics*, August 1969, pp. 247-257.

[80] Merton, Robert C., "Optimal Consumption and Portfolio Rules in a Continuous-Time Model," *Journal of Economic Theory*, December 1971, pp. 373-413.

[81] Merton, Robert C., "An Analytical Derivation of the Efficient Portfolio Frontier," *Journal of Financial and Quantitative Analysis*, September 1972, pp. 1851-1872.

[82] Merton, Robert C., "An Intertemporal Capital Asset Pricing Model," *Econometrica*, September 1973, pp. 867-887.

[83] Merton, Robert C., "On Market Timing and Investment Performance I: An Equilibrium Theory of Value for Market Forecasts," *Journal of Business*, 1981, pp. 363-406.

[84] Merton, Robert C., *Continuous-Time Finance*, 1990, Blackwell Publishers, Cambridge, Massachusetts.

[85] Michaud, Richard O., "The Markowitz Optimization Enigma: Is Optimized Optimal," *Financial Analysts Journal*, January/February 1989, pp. 31-42.

[86] Michaud, Richard O., Efficient Asset Management, 1998, Harvard Business School Press, Boston, Massachusetts.

[87] Nam, Joong-soo, and Ben Branch, "Tactical Asset Allocation: Can It Work?" *Journal of Financial Research*, Winter 1994, pp. 465-479.

[88] von Neumann, J., and O. Morgenstern, *Theory of Games and Economic Behavior*, 2nd edition, 1947, Princeton University Press, Princeton, New Jersey.

[89] Perold, Andre, "Constant Proportion Portfolio Insurance," August 1986, Harvard Business School, working paper.

[90] Perold, Andre, and William F. Sharpe, "Dynamic Strategies for Asset Allocation," *Financial Analysts Journal*, January/February 1988, pp. 16-27.

[91] Philips,Thomas K., Greg T. Rogers, and Robert E. Capaldi, "Tactical Asset Allocation: 1977-1994," *Journal of Portfolio Management*, Fall 1996, pp. 57-64.

[92] Roll, Richard, "A Mean/Variance Analysis of Tracking Error," *Journal of Portfolio Management*, Summer 1992, pp. 13-22.

[93] Rubinstein, Mark, "Continuously Rebalanced Investment Strategies," *Journal of Portfolio Management*, Fall 1991, pp. 78-81.

[94] Samuelson, Paul A., "Lifetime Portfolio Selection by Dynamic Stochastic Programming," *Review of Economics and Statistics*, August 1969, pp. 239-246.

[95] Shanken, Jay, "A Bayesian Approach to Testing Portfolio Efficiency," *Journal of Financial Economics*, 1987, pp. 195-215.

[96] Sharpe, William F., "Integrated Asset Allocation," *Financial Analysts Journal*, September/October 1987, pp. 25-32.

[97] Sharpe, William F., "Investor Wealth Measures and Expected Return," Seminar proceedings from *Quantifying the Market Risk Premium Phenomenon for Investment Decision Making*, The Institute of Chartered Financial Analysts, 1990, pp. 29-37.

[98] Shilling, A. Gary, "Market Timing: Better Than a Buy-and-Hold Strategy," *Financial Analysts Journal*, March/April 1992, pp. 46-50.

[99] Siegel, Jeremy, *Stocks for the Long Run*, 1998, 2nd edition, McGraw-Hill, New York, New York

[100] Solnik, Bruno, "The Relation between Stock Prices and Inflationary Expectations: The International Evidence," *Journal of Finance*, 1983, vol. 38, pp. 35-48.

[101] Stevens, Guy V., "On the Inverse of the Covariance Matrix in Portfolio Analysis," *Journal of Finance*, October 1998, pp. 1821-1827.

[102] Sy, Wilson, "Market Timing: Is It a Folly?" *Journal of Portfolio Management*, Summer 1990, pp. 11-16.

[103] Theil, Henri, *Principles of Econometrics*, 1971, Wiley and Sons, New York, New York.

[104] Treynor, Jack L., and Fisher Black, "How to Use Security Analysis to Improve Portfolio Selection?" *Journal of Business*, January 1973, pp. 66-86.

[105] Trippi, Robert R., and Richard B. Harriff, "Dynamic Asset Allocation Rules: Survey and Synthesis," *Journal of Portfolio Management*, Summer 1991, pp. 19-26.

[106] Vergin, Roger C., "Market-Timing Strategies: Can You Get Rich?" *Journal of Investing*, Winter 1996, pp. 79-86.

[107] Wagner, Jerry, "Why Market Timing Works?" *Journal of Investing*, Summer 1997, pp. 78-81.

[108] Wagner, Jerry, Steve Shellans, and Richard Paul, "Market Timing Works Where it Matters Most ... In the Real World," *Journal of Portfolio Management*, Summer 1992, pp. 86-90.

[109] Weigel, Eric, "The Performance of Tactical Asset Allocation," *Financial Analysts Journal*, September/October 1991, pp. 63-70.

Index

145

Lightning Source UK Ltd.
Milton Keynes UK
UKOW06n0906131116

287464UK00015B/119/P